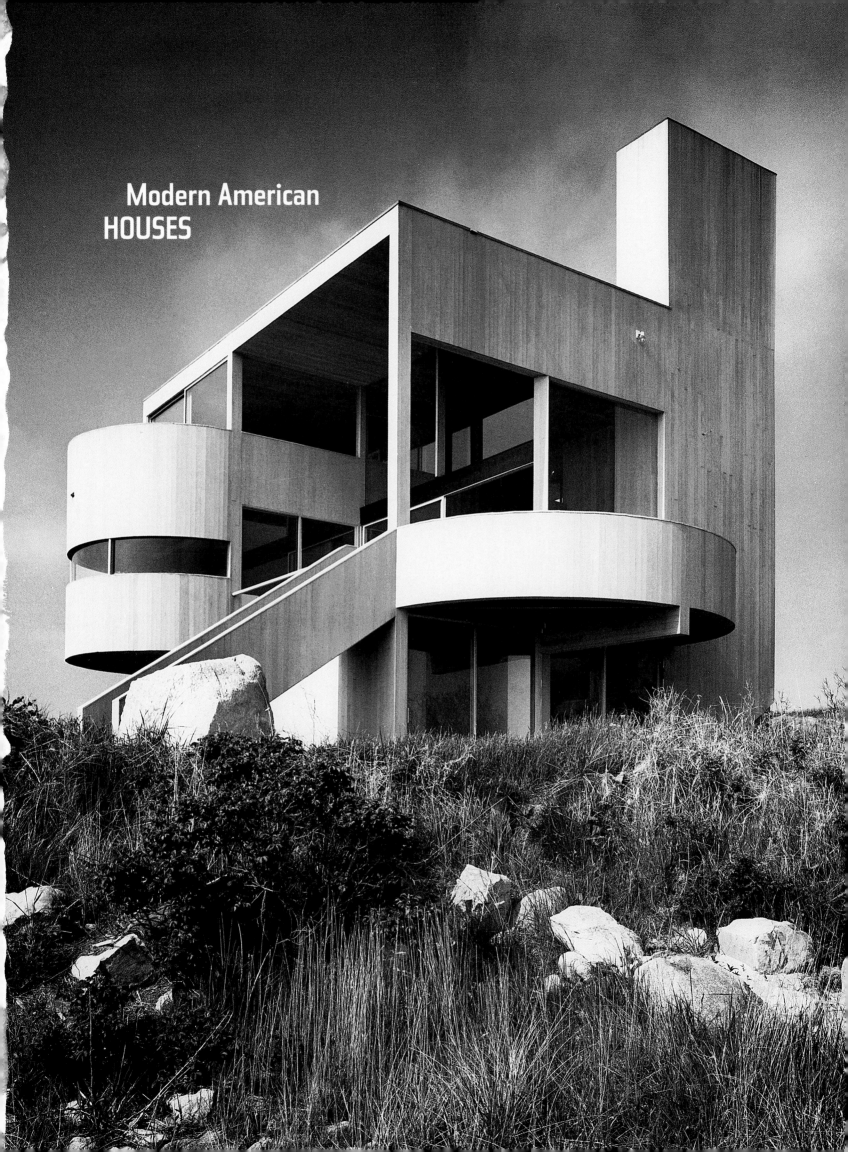

Modern American
HOUSES

Modern American
HOUSES

Four Decades of Award-Winning Design
in ARCHITECTURAL RECORD

EDITED BY

CLIFFORD A. PEARSON

WITH ESSAYS BY

THOMAS HINE,

ROBERT CAMPBELL,

SUZANNE STEPHENS,

AND

CHARLES GANDEE

HARRY N. ABRAMS, INC., PUBLISHERS, IN
ASSOCIATION WITH ARCHITECTURAL RECORD

DENNISON/PEEK HOUSE
MONKTON, VERMONT
BROOKS & CAREY, ARCHITECTS
1992

To **PAUL SACHNER** (1950–1992), who edited *Record Houses* for several years and always had the right words to go with the pictures.

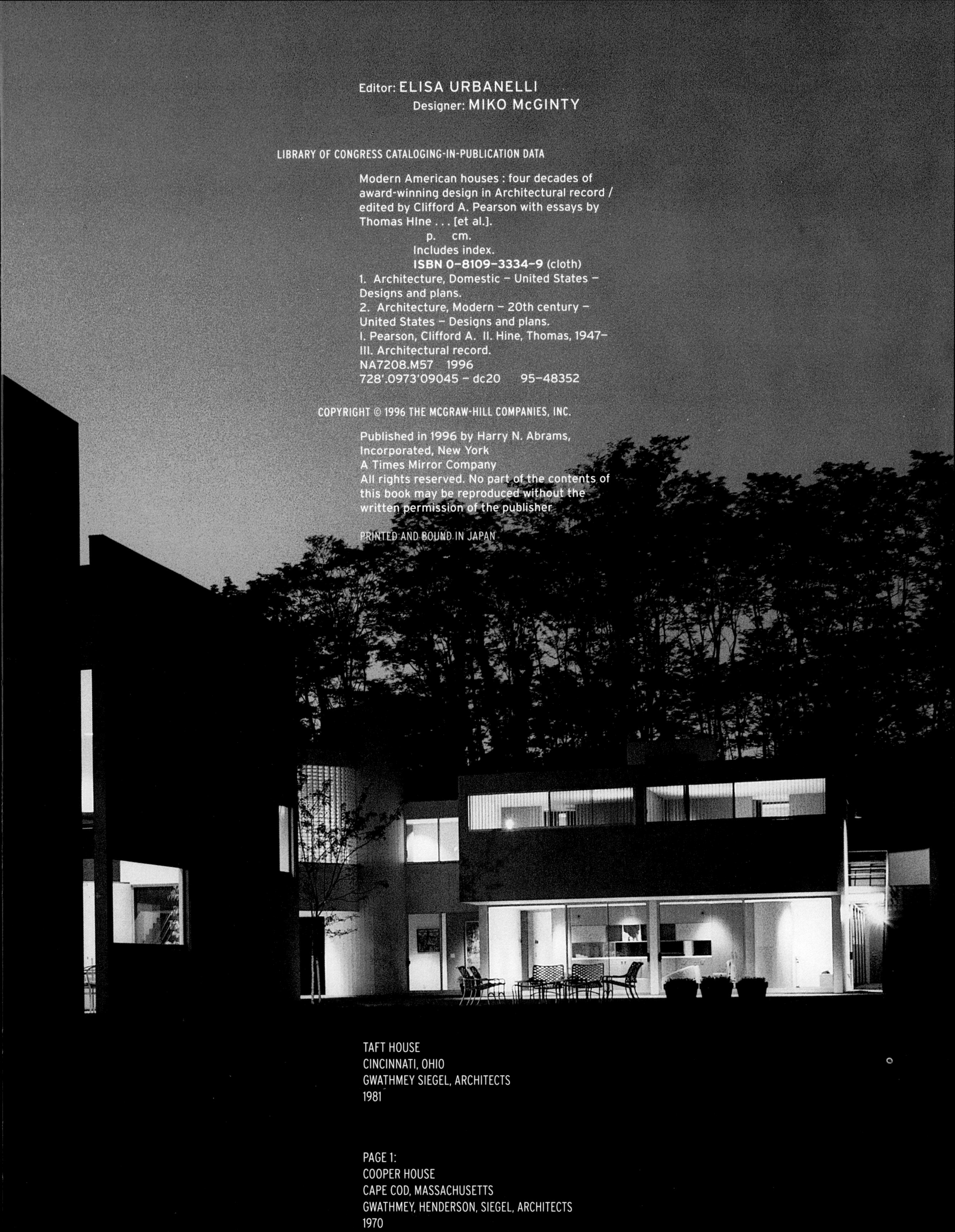

Editor: ELISA URBANELLI
Designer: MIKO McGINTY

LIBRARY OF CONGRESS CATALOGING-IN-PUBLICATION DATA

Modern American houses : four decades of
award-winning design in Architectural record /
edited by Clifford A. Pearson with essays by
Thomas HIne . . . [et al.].
          p.   cm.
Includes index.
ISBN 0–8109–3334–9 (cloth)
1. Architecture, Domestic – United States –
Designs and plans.
2. Architecture, Modern – 20th century –
United States – Designs and plans.
I. Pearson, Clifford A. II. Hine, Thomas, 1947–
III. Architectural record.
NA7208.M57   1996
728'.0973'09045 – dc20   95–48352

COPYRIGHT © 1996 THE MCGRAW-HILL COMPANIES, INC.

Published in 1996 by Harry N. Abrams,
Incorporated, New York
A Times Mirror Company
PRINTED AND BOUND IN JAPAN

TAFT HOUSE
CINCINNATI, OHIO
GWATHMEY SIEGEL, ARCHITECTS
1981

PAGE 1:
COOPER HOUSE
CAPE COD, MASSACHUSETTS
GWATHMEY, HENDERSON, SIEGEL, ARCHITECTS
1970

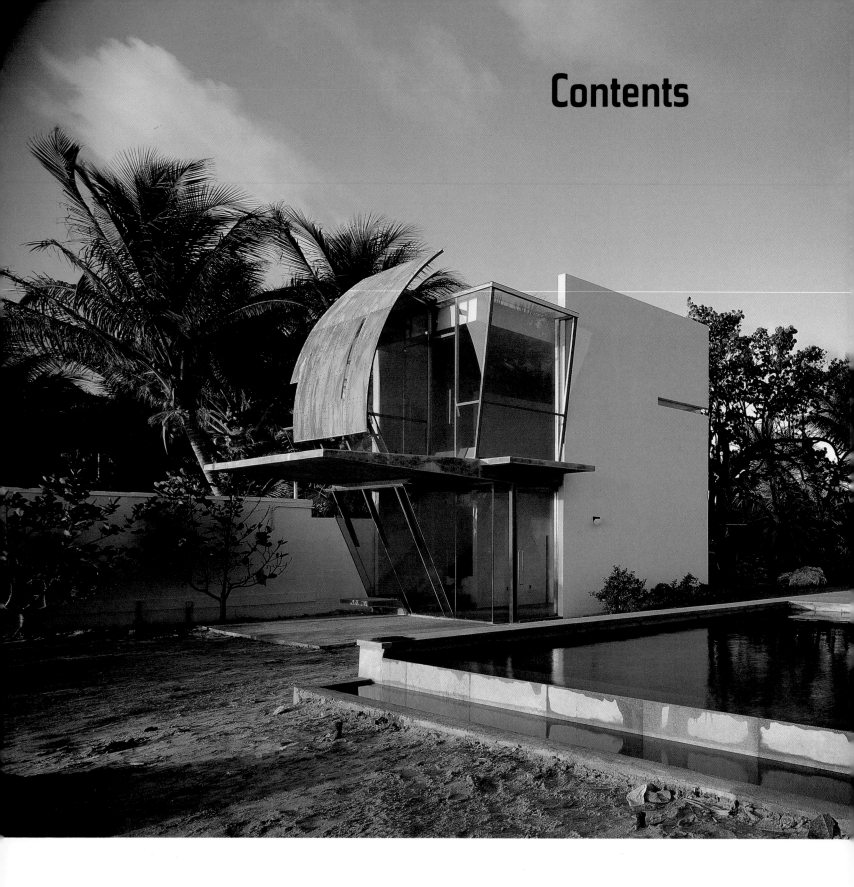

Contents

INTRODUCTION   8

CLIFFORD A. PEARSON

THE 1960S   48

PLAYING BY THE RULES   51
ROBERT CAMPBELL

PORTFOLIO OF HOUSES   58

THE 1950S   12

OF TAILFINS AND BUG SPRAY   15
THOMAS HINE

PORTFOLIO OF HOUSES   22

LANDES HOUSE
GOLDEN BEACH, FLORIDA
CARLOS ZAPATA DESIGN STUDIO AND UNA IDEA,
ARCHITECTS
1994

THE 1970S 100

A TIME OF UPHEAVAL 103
SUZANNE STEPHENS

PORTFOLIO OF HOUSES 112

THE 1980S AND '90S 156

CHIPPING AWAY AT THE
OLD-BOY NETWORK 159
CHARLES GANDEE

PORTFOLIO OF HOUSES 168

LIST OF ALL RECORD HOUSES
BY ARCHITECT 229

CREDITS 234

INDEX 236

Introduction
CLIFFORD A. PEARSON

T-HOUSE
WILTON, NEW YORK
SIMON UNGERS AND TOM KINSLOW, ARCHITECTS
1994

"Do I have to live in a 'statement?' Can't I just have a home?"

Record Houses has long been the most popular issue of *Architectural Record* – a rare hit with both architects and the general public. Nearly every architect designs a house sometime in his or her career and nearly everybody dreams of living in a custom-designed home. So the appeal of this annual publication is understandable. "Each year we sell out the issue on the newsstand," reports Karen Stein, who has been the editor-in-charge of the issue since 1993. "Months after publication, architects published in the issue call to order additional copies and there have been times we have had to say, 'Sorry, no more left.'"

Record Houses also happens to be the issue most likely to elicit angry letters from readers. Each year a few brickbats are tossed at the editors. A recent one declared, "After looking at the 'residences' in *Record Houses* 1995, one wonders where all this nonsense will lead us. Put these houses all together and we have a strange zoo of rare one-of-a-kind animals unable and unwilling to communicate with one another, all doomed to extinction." One can find similar sentiments expressed in letters to the editor almost every year since 1956 when *Record Houses* made its debut as a mid-May special issue. It now runs as the April issue of the magazine. (*Architectural Record* itself dates back much further, to 1891.)

The most common complaint is that the houses in *Record* are oddball designs that serve more as platforms for the architects' own artistic agendas and egos than the needs of their clients. This sentiment was captured perfectly by an Alan Dunn cartoon published in an early issue of *Record Houses*, in which a browbeaten client pleads in vain with his architect, "Do I have to live in a 'statement'? Can't I just have a home?"

Ironically, *Record Houses* began, in part, as a response to a furor in the general press in the mid-1950s over whether modern houses were livable or not. The suburbanization of America was gathering steam, war veterans were starting families, and a bumper crop of houses was being harvested around the country. Builders like William Levitt on Long Island were putting up simple Cape Cods that the burgeoning middle class could afford and feel comfortable with. What were modern architects doing? Designing "statements."

"Hey, what's going on up there?"

steel, open-plan, structurally innovative houses! And if you're as handsome as the Franzens, you can look great doing it.

"The original idea was to show contemporary houses, not just experimental ones," explains Smith. In fact, in the inaugural issue the houses were divided into two categories: twenty examples of contemporary residences designed for "family living" and eight houses with "more adventuresome concepts." Glancing at the two sections today, it's hard to see much of a difference between "contemporary" and "adventuresome." All of the designs were frankly modern, and all explored common themes such as structural innovation, the use of new materials, and the changing relationship between indoors and out. The distinction was dropped the next year and wasn't picked up again. "The innovative houses took over," says Smith.

According to Smith, "*Record Houses* certainly played a part in making modern design more acceptable to a wider audience." With expanded distribution in bookstores and exposure in general readership publications, the annual issue helped non-architects imagine themselves living in modern houses. Of course, this was just one piece of a massive cultural wave linking modernism with progress and the good life. From the new curtain-wall office buildings in which some city people worked to the slim-line telephones on which many housewives talked, modernism pushed its way into the everyday lives of millions of Americans in the 1950s and 1960s.

After the first few years of *Record Houses*, the editors loosened up the cost restrictions, and larger, more expensive homes found their way into the issue. By the 1980s, some truly palatial houses were being shown in *Record Houses*. (Steven Spielberg's residence in East Hampton, designed by Gwathmey Siegel & Associates, and the "farmhouse" in Connecticut by Allan Greenberg are two examples that come immediately to mind. The "farmhouse" takes Mount Vernon as its starting point and then puffs up the scale so the main house is 120 feet long with "attached side pavilions large enough to permit a full-size swimming pool to be within one of them.")

Although such megahouses often leave the biggest impression, they are, in fact, the

"We wanted to show how modern houses were actually lived in," explains Herbert L. Smith, Jr., the first editor of *Record Houses*. Smith had left *Record* in 1954 to be an editor of *Better Homes & Gardens*, but was lured back the next year with the challenge of launching a special annual issue devoted to houses. Like most of the editors then at the magazine, Smith believed in modern design. In his introduction to the first *Record Houses*, Smith wrote that the issue was an extension of the magazine's purpose of "recording and stimulating design progress." Translation: Don't expect to find any neo-Georgian mansions or mock-Colonial residences here.

In the first few issues of *Record Houses*, the editors limited themselves to houses built on budgets falling within a "middle bracket," vaguely defined as permitting "some initiative in design – above the minimum, pared-down budget house, and below the absolute luxury class where economy is not a consideration." Kicking off the initial issue was a house by Ulrich Franzen for his own family. Entitled "The New House For Family Living" by *Record*, the Franzen residence is a dramatic structure with a double-diamond roof deeply cantilevered over twin decks. With three children (two boys, one girl) and, yes, two parents, the Franzens were a classic midcentury suburban American family. The message was clear: If they could live in such a thoroughly modern house, why couldn't everyone else?

Just in case anyone missed the point, Elliott Erwitt, whose photographs had been featured in the popular "Family of Man" exhibit and in *Life* magazine, was commissioned to photograph the Franzens playing, dining, relaxing, and entertaining in their house. See, you *can* live in these glass-and-exceptions, not the rule. Most of the buildings in *Record Houses* are still rather modest, at least in size, especially when compared with today's 4,000- and 5,000-square-foot behemoths erected in upscale subdivisions by speculative builders. One reason *Record* houses tend to be smaller than you might expect is that they are selected for their innovation. In architecture, there often is an inverse relationship between the size of a house and the degree to which it pushes the design envelope. Architects are allowed to be more experimental with smaller projects because the clients tend to be younger, less set in their ways, and more adventurous. Both client and architect must substitute ingenuity and invention for lack of deep pockets.

Looking back on the first decade of *Record Houses*, Smith wrote in 1966, "The real laboratory for inventiveness in architectural design has long been the architect-designed house [as opposed to other types of buildings]. The reasons are many and some are obvious, the ubiquity of houses being not the least of them. Houses are relatively less costly, are built for one client instead of boards or committees, and are designed by almost every architect; indeed the reputations of many architects are founded on significant house designs."

"*Record Houses* was always seen as a celebration of inventiveness," says Douglas Brenner, the editor of *Record Houses* during the first half of the 1980s and now the executive editor of *Garden Design*. But Brenner warns that "houses present a slightly different picture of what's going on in architecture than other, larger building types do. The architect as a visual artist, with all the liberties that such an artist enjoys, is most evident in house design."

Because so many architects get started designing houses (often for their parents), *Record Houses* has served as a launching pad for many a career. Ulrich Franzen remembers the impact of his first *Record* house in 1956. "I was a new kid on the block and getting that house published helped establish me," says Franzen today. *Life* magazine and several other consumer publications picked up the story and Franzen found himself doing television talk shows. Perhaps best of all for a young modernist, Franzen received complimentary letters from both

"Sheer genius! What Pollock did for painting, he's doing for architecture."

"If you can't stand the heat, get out of the Open Plan!"

Walter Gropius and Ludwig Mies van der Rohe after they saw his house in *Record*.

"When we show someone in *Record Houses* who has never been published in a national design magazine, it's our way of saying this is someone to watch," explains current editor Karen Stein. Barclay Gordon, who was the editor of the issue for much of the 1970s, concurs. "*Record Houses* gave young architects the opportunity to spread their wings." Because of this combination of youth and daring, the issue "was always fun to put together," says Gordon.

TRICKLE DOWN, TRICKLE UP

It didn't take long for people in and outside the profession to see *Record Houses* as a

kind of architectural barometer — admittedly imprecise — showing which way the wind was blowing. Who's in? Who's missing? What's hot? The general press often picks up stories from the issue and for many years *The New York Times* regularly showed winning houses in its real estate section.

As a result, the impact of *Record Houses* has been amplified beyond the architectural profession. "It's always fun to see ideas first shown in *Record Houses* turn up in otherwise unremarkable spec houses," says Brenner. "It's usually some superficial motif or element, like the Palladian window, that's picked and then misapplied. Larger ideas dealing with planning or spatial issues take much longer to percolate down, and may, indeed, never really do so."

The trickle-down effect also applies to a few architects themselves. A handful of architects who have been published in *Record Houses* have then gone on to design projects for speculative builders. This short list includes Robert Venturi and Robert A. M. Stern.

A trickle-up effect is even more pronounced. Ideas first seen in *Record Houses* often reappear on a different scale and in mutated form in larger projects such as office buildings, museums, and institutional structures. One can't imagine the commercial buildings of Eric Owen Moss or Joe Valerio without the influence of Frank O. Gehry's residential work, such as the Spiller Houses (1983) or the Norton House (1985). Likewise, the Karas House in Monterey, California, by Charles Moore and William Turnbull (1967) and the "Binker Barn" at Sea Ranch by MLTW/Moore-Turnbull (1973), helped shape an entire generation of regionalist and postmodern architecture.

AND THE WINNERS ARE . . .

While many architectural awards are determined by juries that change each year, *Record Houses* is judged by the editors of the magazine. As a result, there is a continuity in the selection process that is rare for an architectural awards program. "There is a sense of history to it," explains Brenner. "Winners are admitted to a select group that's built from year to year. It's not just what is happening that year. It's a hall of fame of sorts."

In the early years of *Record Houses*, there may have been a consensus on the rightness of modernism. But by the mid-1970s, a multitude of voices was making itself heard in the architectural profession and in the pages of the magazine. "We didn't have a single ideological stance," states Brenner of his tenure at the magazine from 1980 to 1988. Steering clear of "the extremes of being a firebrand" for the latest trend "or a stick-in-the-mud" for the establishment, the editors tried to piece together a balanced picture of architecture. "We tried to show both the vanguard and those who refined existing approaches to design." That approach to selecting winners remains true today.

The architect-client relationship is a key factor in shaping any building, but it is especially important with houses where the client must reveal so much about his or her private way of life. Although they come from various economic strata and different kinds of backgrounds, clients of *Record Houses* do have one thing in common, says Brenner. "They are usually the type of people who want to make a statement with their house."

In its first forty years, *Record Houses* has shown 698 houses and apartments representing nearly every state in America (and a few places outside the country). More than four hundred different architects have had their work presented in the publication; for many of them, it was their first time in the limelight. As its name implies, this annual event has become a record of

residential design, of a changing profession, of evolving attitudes to American lifestyles. In the process, it has become an important part of the ongoing history of architecture.

[Editor's note: The essays introducing each of the four decades were written expressly for this book. The texts accompanying the individual houses, however, were taken from the original issues of Record Houses. *Just as the design of houses changed over the course of four decades, so did the style and format of writing about these houses. Seen in this light, the individual texts are fascinating documents in their own right. However, the layout, selection of photographs, and captions for each story are new and do not try to imitate the design of the original stories.]*

The 1950s

The 1950s: Of Tailfins and Bug Spray

THOMAS HINE

The very first *Record* house, published in 1956, was one that Ulrich Franzen and his wife, referred to only as Mrs. Franzen, planned, designed, and had built for themselves outside of Rye, New York (page 22).

Its plan was simple and symmetrical. A single large space, containing the living and dining areas and the kitchen, was flanked by generous outdoor terraces. Four modest bedrooms were lined up along the back. It was a relatively small house on a two-acre, mostly wooded plot.

For this first house, *Record* chose to go beyond conventional architectural photographs and supplement them with views, by the distinguished photographer Elliott Erwitt, of Franzen and his family actually inhabiting the house. These scenes of what we weren't yet calling the nuclear family were intended to reinforce the argument of the accompanying essay by A. Lawrence Kocher. The essay was an exercise in post–World War II romantic rationalism – the faith that the path to freedom is through analysis. The house is said to be the result of rigorous thinking about the family's needs and desires over time.

The fascination of this layout to a reader encountering it today lies in the complete mismatch of the house itself and the terms available to discuss it. We look at the house today and see fantasy, and arrogance, and expansiveness. We see a graphic image so strong it could be a corporate logo. It's a product of America at its most lovable and crass. Yet the essay, grounded in Gropius with overtones of Freud, is an exercise in analytical alchemy – an effort to turn the arbitrary into the inevitable.

Kocher was able to look at a plan as symmetrical and diagrammatic, though hardly as subtle, as anything by Palladio and see it as an expression of modern fluidity and a break with tradition. And Erwitt's candid glimpses of a little girl and a dalmatian, of woodland peeking over the kitchen counter, of the owners and guests sharing a salad at the dining table were intended to underscore Kocher's argument that modernism is not simply good to look at, but good for you as well.

For Kocher, as for the many advocates of modern domestic architecture who preceded and followed him, the open plan expressed freedom, an acceptance of change, a concern with child welfare, an embrace of technology, and a pragmatic, yet poetic response of a society tested by Depression and war to the realities of family life without servants.

"Future art historians will probably speak of the mid-decades of the twentieth century as a time of artistic rebellion and change," Kocher wrote. "It is now, during these years, that we have come to accept change and disown our artistic inheritance. We try to avoid the stigma of being considered traditional or followers of the cliché."

In eschewing the old clichés, architects inevitably embraced the clichés of their own time. Quite a few jump out of these first four issues of *Record Houses*: sculptural, freestanding fireplaces, the "Japanese" gardens, the same dozen chairs in what could be the same glass-walled room in Oregon, Florida, Minnesota, or Connecticut.

In nearly every case, the architect is praised for his originality and innovation. Admitting one's influences was not yet fashionable. But forty years later, the sense of consensus is overwhelming. One house flows into another as seamlessly as the kitchen empties into the dining area which then swells into the living room. Browsing these houses puts the reader in such a horizontal state of mind that when, in a house published in 1958, George Nelson and Gordon Chadwick remind us that a staircase can organize and energize an architectural space, it comes as a bit of a shock.

There are, in fairness, a number of buildings that do stand out. Some so thoroughly distill the ideas that were in the air that they're somehow definitive. For example, the Malibu beach house Craig Ellwood designed for Dr. and Mrs. Victor M. Hunt is

OPPOSITE:
A ROOF OVER ONE'S HEAD: FAMILY LIFE AT THE FRANZEN HOUSE, CIRCA 1956, AS CAPTURED BY PHOTOGRAPHER ELLIOTT ERWITT.

PRECEDING PAGES:
BEATTIE HOUSE
RYE, NEW YORK
ULRICH FRANZEN, ARCHITECT
1958

A ROOF OVER ONE'S CAR: THE COHEN HOUSE, DESIGNED BY PAUL RUDOLPH, RESPONDS TO THE FLORIDA CLIMATE WITH BREEZEWAYS AND A CARPORT, RATHER THAN ENCLOSED SPACES.

so austere, so exposed, and so silent, one feels that a house cannot be any less than this.

Other houses represent alternatives that went unexplored in the culture at large. In 1958 and 1959, there was an interest in houses within walled courts, most notably a feature on the Cambridge, Massachusetts, home of José Luis Sert (page 44), which was given an Elliott Erwitt photo spread similar to that of the Franzen house. Fences were, and remain, a contentious issue in the suburbs. Although their advocates argued that high barriers make a place for freedom and privacy, the consensus was that fences are somehow un-American.

There are heavy houses – habitable sculptures made from concrete – and light ones on stilts that seem reluctant to settle down. The best of them have a matter-of-fact quality, a sense that modernity is not a cause, but a condition.

Obviously *Record* houses were not typical, nor did anyone claim that they were. The decade of the 1950s utterly transformed the American landscape and filled it with houses that, like the *Record* houses, sought informality and "togetherness," but whose marks of prestige were not the same ones taught at the Harvard Graduate School of Design. Like most consumer products, the typical developer's house was a bundle of salable features – a picture window, a tiled bath, a finished rec room, an all-electric kitchen – rather than an integrated whole. On the outside, such houses wore badges of rustic domesticity, such as a bit of split-rail fence, and sported modest porticoes or pediments that referred not so much to classicism as to patriotism and Early American forebears. The typical house was a recognizable package: a ranch, a Cape Cod, a split-level, a garrison Colonial. But whether traditional or contemporary, their plans were quite similar.

As in almost any selection of this type, *Record Houses* offers more revealing period pieces than timeless masterpieces, and that's a large part of its usefulness. Unrepresentative as the houses may be of the places where most Americans lived, they are, nevertheless, revealing of the way in which mainstream modernist architects thought about the freestanding, single-family home, and its context – or lack of it.

The setting of nearly all the early *Record* houses was the unspoiled suburb at convenient driving distance from the office. In the pages of the magazine, they seem to exist in some prelapsarian state of nature, without neighbors or any evidence of a larger community.

Now that we're playing the role of those future historians Kocher anticipated, the rebellion and ferment he thought we'd see in the Franzen House isn't readily apparent. And because we see Mrs. Franzen only in the kitchen and in the dining room serving food, we might doubt that open planning by itself causes a breakdown of outmoded social relationships.

Moreover, most of the elements touted as new and important in the Franzen house – expression of its steel structure, the use of movable, nonstructural partitions in an open plan, and walls of windows – had been around for quite a while by 1956. Those that didn't derive from European modernism of thirty years before came from Frank Lloyd Wright, who had been around forever.

Offhandedly, Kocher did mention one thing that helps explain a lot about the house and its time. Noting that the building is on a wooded site and that the two terraces are open at their sides, he explained that screens weren't necessary because Franzen regularly sprayed insecticides throughout the grounds. Rachel Carson hadn't yet written *Silent Spring*, and most people were not aware of any danger from insecticides. But it nevertheless seems significant that an architect should be praised for forgoing an architectural solution – screens – and using chemicals instead.

The fantasy that underlies this house, and many others of its period, is that it's possible in the suburbs to have unmediated contact with nature. The second-growth forest in which so many of these houses were built lacked the implicit meaning of either urban sites or well-defined agricultural landscapes. The architect could see himself making a small, indeed absurd, gesture in an indifferent environment. Or he could imagine his work ordering the environment and embracing nature as yet another part of modern living.

Screens can have wonderful architectural qualities. But they do, however softly, acknowledge limits. And just as Franzen and other architects of his time were reluctant to acknowledge that some activities happen better in rooms of their own, they also sought to deny that black flies are a more natural part of the forest than upper middle-class householders.

Architects often like to pretend that they control more than they do. (It's part of the same disease that turns writers about architecture into social critics.) But there is something poignant about the thought of an architect systematically poisoning his land so that he won't have to do what architects have always done – design a wall.

And why didn't he want to design a wall? You know the answer because, like anyone who reads an architectural magazine or a book like this one, you've looked at the pictures first: He had designed a roof.

The key picture in *Record*'s layout of the Franzen house was a head-on view, photographed by Ezra Stoller, that showed the double-diamond roof structure apparently floating above the house. This roof and the structure that supports it, rather than any functional analysis, seem to have generated the house's plan. Moreover, it almost certainly generated the magazine's interest in the house.

In order for the house to present the dynamic image that was sought, it had to float free at its outer edges. That's the reason for the symmetrical pair of shaded terraces. Placement of screens on the front or side of one or both of the terraces might have made them more functional, but it would have compromised the cantilever. Instead of soaring, the house would seem to be hobbling about on crutches.

The roof is the thing about the house that most captures the sense of its time. This was, after all, the age of the tailfin, an era when modernity was expressed in ever more baroque ways. Speed and excitement, which had previously been evoked by rounded streamlined forms, were now embodied in the acute-angled forms inspired by jet fighter planes. Architects strived to prevent their creations from appearing earthbound.

The way we see the roof today is colored by subsequent events. A similar, though far less elegant, roof profile soon became a familiar fixture of the commercial landscape. It was used on A&W Root Beer stands, and sundry other roadside attractions. That low-culture association somewhat tarnishes the Franzen House as a serious architectural statement, even as it makes it a more expressive pop icon.

The hot dog and soda sellers didn't miss the point. This diamond roof profile is instantly recognizable. It draws a second look, and a third. It has pizzazz – a quality that was not discussed in *Record*'s essay on the Franzen house, but which comes through quite clearly in the photographs.

The resemblance between the architect's house and the roadside building remains troublesome. It's easy to understand why a fast-food chain would decide to erect an eye-catching building that stands out in the placeless environment of the highway strip. But why would a rising young architect build such an image for his family to inhabit? In the great tradition of houses architects build for themselves, it was a way to get attention. And with the massive abandonment of the city as a place to live, the architect became less concerned with how it looked on the street than how it read in a photograph. Deprived both of settings in which their buildings would have meaning and of traditions within which they could express themselves, architects had little choice but to produce flashy attention-getting packages.

The Franzen House had the architectural equivalent of automobile tailfins, and for much the same reason cars did. Tailfins were, according to Harley Earl, the General Motors styling chief usually credited with inventing them, a visual receipt for the buyer's extra money. It's no accident that tailfins became almost universal during the late 1950s, or that there was a great interest in more elaborate houses with strong imagery. Each year, the *Record* houses seemed, as a group, to become larger. The same thing was happening for most other American houses as well, as a result of powerful economic and demographic trends, along with very effective marketing.

As Kocher noted in his discussion of the Franzen House, memories of the Great Depression and fear of its repetition helped shape houses of the era. He argued that the recollection of hard times made houses more practical, with less money invested in needless rooms and ornament. Today, we're more likely to see the entire roof as a kind of ornament, one that adds drama and romance to an otherwise unadorned house. It's obviously more than just a roof over one's head.

And it was built at a moment when Americans were able and willing to spend money on expressive objects and houses. In contrast, the first decade after World War II had been a period of practicality. Levittown-type suburban housing developments may not have been modern in style, but they surely represented a rather more rigorous analysis of people's perceived needs and the most efficient way of providing them than did the Franzen House. These subdivision houses did what architects claimed to do, only better and more cheaply. They did lack beauty, of course, but architects didn't talk much about that either.

"We have yet to prove that a democracy can produce a beautiful environment," huffed architect Edward Durrell Stone in a 1959 *New York Times Magazine* article, "The Case Against the Tailfin Age." Stone particularly condemned the informal, open-planned house, as "a good excuse for laziness: it is transparently easier to feed children in the back yard – like ranch hands – than it is to have them seated at a table behaving like potentially civilized adults."

Yet Stone understood better than most architects the value of adding some luxurious, eye-catching architectural element to his buildings – such as the concrete screens and reflecting pools on his United States Pavilion at the 1958 Brussels World's Fair and at the American Embassy in New Delhi – to make them more memorable and desirable.

As 1955 approached, business leaders and economists were worried. By then, nearly all Americans would have caught up with their consumption after the Depression and war, and the generation coming to the prime age of household formation – the Depression babies – was small because of the extremely low birthrate of that period. Could this be the bust at the end of the postwar boom?

It wasn't, of course. Per capita income was rising far more dramatically than the cost of living, and Americans became persuaded to "move up," to spend more on each item they bought in order to acquire

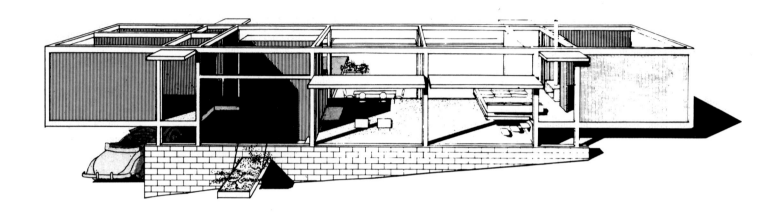

APPLEBEE HOUSE
AUBURN, ALABAMA
PAUL RUDOLPH, ARCHITECT
1956

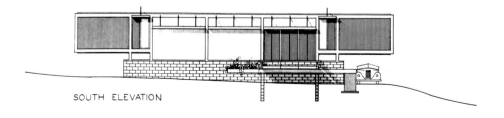

SOUTH ELEVATION

greater convenience, more prestige, and an air of excitement. You may not sell more houses, but you could sell more house to each buyer.

As Russell Lynes noted in the 1957 edition of *Record Houses*, people were viewing their homes as consumer goods, "built as much to move out of as to move into." Architects, he said, tend to take a static, European view of their buildings, while those who inhabit them behave as nomads. He said the house had become a stepping-stone on an incessant journey and that the houses themselves were expressing this sense of restlessness. "Indeed some of the houses in this issue of the *Record* seem to be in motion themselves, hovering just above the ground, not on it, as though they might flap their wings and migrate at any moment."

And speaking of the deep-seated, "butterfly" sling chairs found in so many *Record* houses, and everywhere else, Lynes wrote, "We don't expect anyone to make a family seat out of a Hardoy chair," evoking the name of the chair's designer. But an estimated 5 million such chairs, most of them knockoffs, were sold during the 1950s. An ad in *House and Garden* asked $7.45 for the "deluxe model" and $14.95 for the "authentic model." These chairs had a lightness and a sense of modernity that was very attractive to a wide public. They had a structural expressiveness that we see echoed in the Franzen house and many other early *Record* houses. Those who commissioned an architect-designed house expected a powerful image, which most often meant an adventurous structural profile.

One thing that is evident as the decade went on is increasing size. The Franzen House might have been conceptually limitless, but its floor area was relatively modest, and its bedrooms and baths almost ascetic. But a year or two later, houses were more like compounds, or even hamlets, with living wings, children's wings, and utility wings, linked in a few cases by bridges and in others, more daringly, by outdoor courtyards. The architects were not only finding ways to spend the owners' obviously lavish budgets. They were building simulacra of urban communities on single-family plots.

Meanwhile, in the real world, a variety of new housing "products" were being rolled out to soak up additional family income: the split-level, the raised ranch, the family room, even the fallout shelter. We became addicted to physical expansiveness.

Our houses have continued to grow even when our incomes have not, along with roads, parking lots, and the other construction that supports such sprawl. By 1990, there was twice as much developed land for each American as there had been in 1955, after the first wave of mass suburbanization.

Architects have not shaped much of this physical expansion, whose impact has been to create environments where architecture has little relevance or impact. We look to the architect for little more than a memorable image. You can't really live in an image, of course. But as the Franzen House reminds us, insecticide helps.

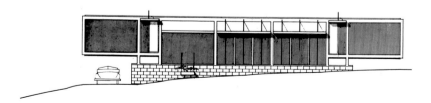

NORTH ELEVATION

Franzen House
Westchester County, New York
Ulrich Franzen, Architect
1956

The New House For Family Living

A HOUSE THAT IS LIVED IN

We have chosen in these first few pages, to break with tradition in architectural publication, to show one of our selected houses as occupied by a family. Our illustrations are of its living, dining, and play areas, in actual use. The Ulrich Franzens, who developed and built the house, were photographed with the interior as a background. They appear as normally concerned with routine activities: caring for children, preparation of food, dining, entertaining guests, and relaxing.

Mr. Franzen is an architect, Harvard trained, whose ideas for the house were supported and aided by his wife, a Bennington College graduate. The two spent several months in setting up space needs for their family of three children (a girl and two boys) plus a dog and a cat.

The design objective was to create a house for their particular family, one that gave promise of lasting usefulness and attraction. "Not a place," observed Mrs. Franzen, "that was sterile of ideas, soon to be outmoded and outlived—soon to become the nightmare, as to 'The Man in the Gray Flannel Suit.'" It was a requirement of the plan that there be space throughout the house for the effective display of a varied collection of contemporary art, consisting of murals, small paintings, and sculpture.

The site was selected after a long search by auto excursions in three states bordering New York City, where the architect has his office. The two-acre plot, on which the house is placed, is thickly wooded and has rugged outcroppings of stone. An ancient stone wall borders one side of the property. Because of the nature of the ground and a preference for the natural setting, there was no need for formal planting and an expanse of lawn, difficult to maintain.

The house is two miles from the town of Rye, New York, and three-quarters of an hour commuting time from Manhattan. There are nursery and public schools nearby; a bathing beach and boat basin on Long Island Sound are within a short walking distance.

We consider the Franzen House, shown on these opening pages, to be a fair example of the sort of domestic design that is being contrived today by an enthusiastic group of young architects whose training, since the Second World War, has stressed and applied the theoretical and experimental. The nature of its light steel roof framing, the manner in which the outer enclosing walls and inner partitions are completely independent of the structural frame, the wide selection of factory fabricated units, along with the large sheets of plate glass and insulation panels—all make us aware of a new approach to design and a skillfully contrived shaping of construction. Industrial production, as here, is playing an increasing part in current efforts by architects of energy and creative ambition.

The house as architecture has a quality that is quite different from that to which we have long been accustomed, looking back a decade or more. We must admit that occasionally we are startled by its daring, but, at the same time, vastly stimulated by the courageous effort that is being exerted in order to avoid any semblance of the century-long practice of copying ideas of others or style borrowing from the past. We can fittingly quote Gauguin here, who said that in art there are only revolutionists and plagiarists. If architects at this moment are appearing to be in revolt, it is with a sense of gain for the future, since all movements that have taken place in the past for the improvement of architecture, have been preceded by revolt.

Future art historians will probably speak of the mid-decades of the twentieth century as a time of artistic rebellion and change. It is now, during these years, that we have come to accept change and disown our artistic inheritance. We try to avoid the stigma of being considered traditional or followers of the cliché. The old stylistic standards which for centuries were the measuring stick for judging architecture are at this time definitely neglected or outmoded. That architect is an exceptional rarity who would suggest to a client that a proposed house for an American suburb be given a Colonial, Spanish, or French Provincial look. Even the current ranch house rage can be considered a cloak covering a free-flowing, if emaciated, non-stylistic manner. A dissenting architect called it "modern in sheep-ranch clothing"!

AGE OF EXPERIMENTATION

In the face of this recognized design upheaval, it is natural that we look for the causes. A part of the origin of the upheaval—some would call it a revolution—can be traced to a chastening influence

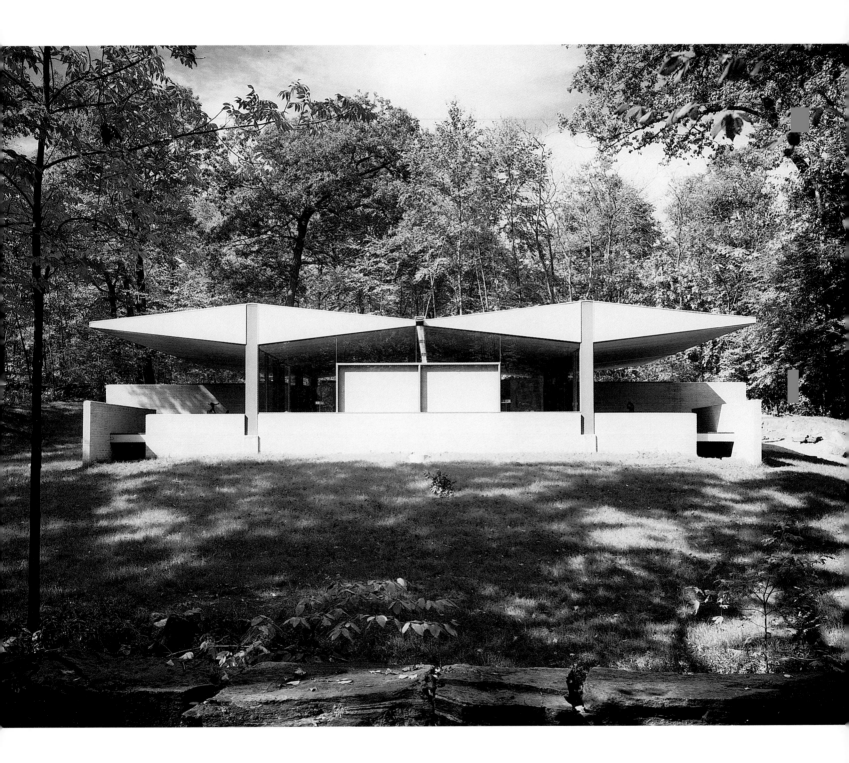

of the depression of the '30s. We see plainly a decline in the century-long domination of "style" taking place gradually as a consequence of stringent conditions during the early depression years. There was an extreme necessity for economy at the time. Housing was an urgent need, yet almost none was provided. In order to cut costs, building forms were greatly simplified; elaborate doorways, denticulated cornices, and Spanish ironwork were banished from domestic work. Among the mementoes of these years were a countrywide rash of Tom Thumb golf courses and the equally widespread Drive-in Overnight Cabins—forerunners of the deluxe motels of today.

These stimulants to recovery were not jobs for the architect,

even though they represented our single, but brief building boom. Architects, during the lull, became interested in low-cost housing; some dabbled in prefabrication. Experimentation was taking place by both architects and industry. New materials and novel construction methods were turned to as a means of cutting costs. Among the new materials introduced were fiber and press-boards, plywood, asbestos-cement products, plastics of an early kind, aluminum and other metals. Houses with steel frame, faced with panels of standard widths, others of plywood, canvas surfaced, precast concrete units, and porcelain-enameled steel walls were announced for marketing, although almost none reached a mass production stage. These

happenings were among the evidences of a disrupted architectural practice.

A second cause leading to change in the nature and aims of architectural practice can be attributed to altered teaching methods of architectural schools. The use of the Orders of Architecture as the *vade mecum* for imparting good proportion and a vocabulary of architecture, was gradually given up. Most of the accredited schools cease to bend the knee or do homage to the Ecole des Beaux-Arts in Paris. Back in 1924 George Bernard Shaw, in a letter to *Architectural Record* in response to a questionnaire concerning the training of the architect, anticipated the coming change in teaching when he said tartly that:

Architects are made by building, not by books.... [T]he more an architect knows academically, the worse he builds. Reading, picture-gazing, and globe trotting all tend to shift an architect's eyes to the back of his head.

At the height of the so-called teaching change, shortly after 1936, Walter Gropius, a distinguished teacher and founder of the German Bauhaus, was brought to Harvard and placed in the charge of courses in the school of design. He soon attracted to this country his Bauhaus aides, Mies van der Rohe, Joseph Albers, Marcel Breuer, Herbert Bayer, Howard Dearstyne, and L. Moholy-Nagy. All of these Bauhaus associates, without exception, found places in architectural schools. They, with many others in the profession, were to turn the attention of America to one of our most fruitful and typical resources, namely mass production and standardization. We may hesitate to accept the utilitarian Ford factory and the supermarket villages as possessing aesthetic qualities, but we can welcome the clear evidence of arrival at a freer, more original

and imaginative interpretation of the house as it is being experimentally produced today for American family living.

CURRENT TRENDS IN HOUSE DESIGN

As we leaf over the accompanying pages to form a preliminary impression of current offerings in house design, we become aware that the long-familiar oversized and traditional *country house*, set back from the limits of the property, usually alongside a formal garden, is now seemingly obsolete. Increased building costs and taxation have taken care of that. Houses built now are manifestly suburban and informal in character. They are far less pretentious and extravagant; more significantly, they are outwardly a

logical expression of our industrial age and of our American manner of living.

The contemporary house has a "new look." It consists of a more open grouping of rooms, usually all on one floor. Its facing of masonry and weatherboarding has been largely replaced by the window wall and, in some instances, by a complete encirclement of glass. In addition, a new system of fabrication is being introduced that makes use of a steel or wood framework, and has an infilling of glass or factory-made panels. It is obvious from our illustrations that the architect of today has become more daring, and more, what we may term, "industrial minded"; his methods of construction are more technical and complicated than those a generation ago. Newer building operations require a close partnership of architect, engineer, and industry. The combination of steel, glass, plastics, and other materials makes it urgently necessary that all parts be fitted together as a delicate and complex mechanism.

Returning to our review of current houses, we can perceive here and there the novelty of a frankly revealed structural skeleton. Vertical supports on the surface of the house are modularly spaced with a regularity that produces a pleasant wall pattern similar to the outer facing of a Japanese house. There is, as we know from

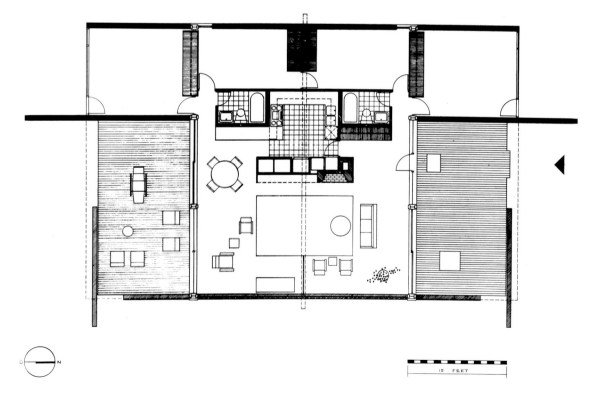

oriental examples, an aesthetic attraction in a revealed structure. Mies van der Rohe, who applies this system for dwellings, has succeeded in creating wall units that are attractive by their patterning and rhythm. August Perret in France has, of course, been using reinforced concrete as the bare bones of his buildings since 1900, with interstices filled with concrete or brick.

Among our illustrations there are instances of freestanding walls, often placed at right angles to one another. The purpose of these walls, as with the Franzen House, is largely nonstructural, and may serve as a termination of a terrace, producing a subdivision in the adjacent garden.

Partitions within the house have been undergoing a transformation of purpose. Instead of being rigidly fixed and supporting, they are now often flexible and movable to a new location. They sometimes extend upward to a height not exceeding an easy reach, that is, just above the sight lines. Closets, organized with subdivisions for trays, racks, shelves, and hanging rods, are occasionally installed as a means for subdividing, either temporarily or permanently, the entire area of a house floor.

ELECTRONICS AND LACK OF SERVANTS INFLUENCE DESIGN

Most American homes are now maidless, so kitchen and dining habits are being subjected to change. The house that is without benefit of maid or laundress naturally becomes a haven for every possible labor-saving and automatic device. This lack of permanent help has brought on a heyday of gadgetry.

"Electronics," if that is the word, are making over our living space, and remolding our daily home life. In the house, of this 1955–56 model, we are rather sure to find television, radio, a Hi-Fi record player, a tape recorder, film projector, a device to waken us in the morning and to sing us to sleep at night, plus a variety of automatic controls for opening ventilators and controlling temperature. Lewis Mumford, in pondering over these aids to living,

seems to intimate that a time might arrive when, as in Butler's *Erewhon*, mechanical invention will become a crime and machines will be assigned to the museum as a warning to the human race! At the same time, these have certainly brought more comfort and convenience to the American house.

The nature of this suburban house and its plan provisions are shaped directly by family habits and activities: hobbies, entertaining of friends around the terrace grill, weekend parties, Cub Scout meetings, and gardening. Other plan features have sprung from principles of child welfare, such as a combined library and mechanical workroom varied with the advancement of the child. The trend of including both a family

room and a separate living room also reflects this thinking.

Outdoor life, along with the desire for sunshine and recreation, is also contributing to the reshaping of the house, giving us game rooms and terraces for leisurely sitting and sunbathing. The basement playroom has often been brought up to the first floor because its former location was inconvenient, and difficult for the mother's supervision of young children. The same is the case with the heater room and laundry. These are dignified by a ground-level position, sometimes placed as an adjunct of the kitchen, and, at the same time, convenient to a service yard, screened by shrubbery from the garden terrace. A workshop may become an annex to the garage

or carport. The do-it-yourself fad has given us a first-aid bar as a replacement for our first-aid kit!

There is a familiar vocabulary associated with modern design indicative of a changing manner of building. Some of the descriptive terms are fluidity of space, rational structural system, cantilever support, prefabricated units, modular panels, and shed, undulating, and butterfly roofs. The "picture window" is becoming an almost obsolete term, in the wake of the side-sliding, ball-bearing, floor-to-ceiling sash. The wide projecting eaves, to shield the house from intense southern sun, have practical meaning for the air-conditioned home. Floor surfaces have been improved by the introduction of materials that retain their gloss, even with hard

usage, and that require little or no polishing. Houses placed on a site with a gentle slope are sometimes designed with what is termed a "split-level," which, like split personalities, may have their own peculiar attraction.

It is not unusual today to have rooms with controlled openings to the sky, at the center of the house. Screens to windows can now be raised or lowered by push-button control. Experiments are being made to improve the use of screening; some have even proposed abolishing all screening by the substitution of periodical applications of insect-repelling spray around the house and at all windows and doors. This is now being applied at the Franzen House. Increased interior daylight has encouraged the planting of

shrubs indoors. This is favored, not alone for appearance, but also to contribute to the maintenance of a healthful humidity level.

If we were to summarize the more noticeable and hopeful tendencies in domestic design by architects of the past year, recognition would be made of the gradual acceptance of new building processes and factory-produced materials. Herein lies a new esthetic and an indigenous quality. There is also a promise of adding enrichment and authenticity to our national architecture. While originality was the least of the virtues that the architect of the nineteenth century wished to possess, it becomes the aim and the goal of his twentieth-century successor.

A. Lawrence Kocher, 1956

COHEN HOUSE

Contemporary materials and techniques often go a long way toward helping produce the "most house for the least money." This light and airy house on Siesta Key, Sarasota, Florida, is composed almost entirely of prefabricated parts. It is quite spacious—and of moderate cost.

Besides the wide variety of manufactured items commonly used in houses today, architect Paul Rudolph has also employed ready-made girders and panels for the walls and roof. The panels are of a "sandwich" construction, with a honeycomb core of phenolic-impregnated paper, and hardboard or plywood of various types glued to either side; they resist fire, decay, and termites, and are lightweight enough to serve as sliding doors in several locations. The girders span thirty-two feet across the living room and are of a "stressed-skin" type, formed of plywood glued to light wood members.

The roof is constructed in two levels, with the upper one supported atop the beams. The lower roof panels project six feet into the room and are suspended from the beams; to the outside, they project as a four-foot overhang, either cantilevered or attached by pins to sides of wooden posts. Spaces between beams form a clerestory for extra light and air.

The Neighborhood: Sarasota, on the west coast of Florida, is a quiet, sun-drenched land of palms and palmettos with a balmy climate.

The Site: Ample in size and level, the lot adjoins a bayou and abounds in tropical trees and

foliage. An artificial inlet has been made in the bayou to bring it to the perimeter of the house at the back.

The Family: Mr. and Mrs. David Cohen are an extremely musical couple. He is concert master for the Florida West Coast Symphony, and she is a pianist. They wanted a house that would accommodate large groups for rehearsals and recitals, and with good acoustics and sound system. From the design standpoint, they asked for a simple, straightforward, practical house that required a minimum of housekeeping.

The House: The plan of the house works ideally for informal, servantless living, as well as the family's specific requirements. By

eliminating all partitions except those of the bedrooms and baths, an enormous multipurpose living area was created for entertaining and orchestra practice sessions. Even the kitchen is a part of the room; cabinets are arranged to shield the actual cooking processes from view. Sliding windows and doors join terraces at the front and back to the living area.

Large closets and a dressing room (well lighted by overhead skylights) minimize the need for excess furniture in the bedrooms, permitting them to be used as sitting rooms on occasion.

The Architect: Paul Rudolph remarks, "Perhaps the most interesting feature of the house is the sunken area in the living room which is surrounded by cushions

on the floor and additional cushions for back supports. We are much interested in the simplification and elimination of furniture and this seems to be a step. We feel strongly that too much modern furniture is so sculpturesque that it is difficult to make a truly quiet room."

Owner's Reaction: The Cohens muse, "The house is right. Not fancy—very ample and straightforward—practical—not ornate—no lost space, NONE— no silly walls with curves or dead-end rooms."

1956

Kirkpatrick House

In a time when the horizontal line reigns in house design, it is intriguing to note here how much visual spaciousness can be added by vistas looking up as well as across and out. A good sense of scale is given, too, by contrasting the verticals and horizontals. It is an interesting house, pervaded by an air of quiet elegance and warmth. Day and night, carefully planned lighting adds a touch of sparkle and drama to the interiors.

The plan organization and use of durable materials add up to good livability. The first-floor plan centers on a multipurpose dining/family room, used somewhat like the traditional English "hall." An entrance vestibule with coat closet opens directly into it, as does the garage. The living room forms a quiet area at the end of the house. Upstairs, a children's wing is set apart with a large playroom. The house is

Kirkpatrick House
Kalamazoo, Michigan
George Nelson and Gordon
Chadwick, Architects
1958

wood frame, with concrete foundations and exterior walls of ribbed aluminum panels.

Artificial light, used as a device to explain and heighten design features, is worth notice in this house. All too often, the utilitarian niceties of lighting are the only ones given much consideration in residential design. Here, light is used as well to create an atmosphere within and without the house, and to re-create at night all the focal points around the two-story wells. By using only the exterior lights in the overhangs, soft illumination is provided inside; a series of lights along the stairwell give utilitarian light and dramatize that feature; and with all lights on, a brilliant "party atmosphere" is created.

Ceiling edges and lights are recessed where there are no actual vertical wells to give the same effect. Storage walls in the living room and the well are lighted in a fashion to give soft background glow. Activity areas in the multipurpose room are defined by pools of light over tables and sofas.

1958

Bridge House

This idyllic house blends two strong, yet often quite divergent trends: a rational, regulated neo-Palladian influence dominates the plan and balanced design; a decided romantic turn is obvious in the setting, bridgelike construction, vaulted roof, terra-cotta-colored stucco exterior (patterned with bas-reliefs)—and gargoyles for downspouts.

The central, glassed-in living pavilion is flanked by four masonry square wings, one at each corner. These wings zone the house for its various functions. One provides for servant's room, kitchen, and laundry. Another has three family bedrooms and a bath. A third has the master bedroom, dressing room, and bath. The fourth contains a study/guest room, powder room, and a quiet, walled-in court. The wings have flat roofs and nine-foot-high ceilings, while the dominant central "living bridge" has three arches rising thirteen feet from the floor. Finishes throughout are rich in tone: gold leaf on the vaulted ceiling, terrazzo floors, ebonized wood cabinets.

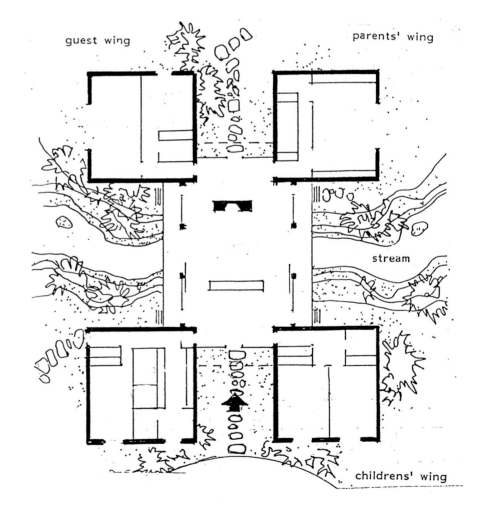

guest wing

parents' wing

stream

childrens' wing

Although this house would be effective in any setting, the one in which it is placed highly dramatizes the central living pavilion. This unit is built as a simple steel and concrete bridge over the quiet, shallow stream that meanders through the property. The wings and retaining walls anchor it firmly, visually and in reality, to the banks of the stream. Sliding glass doors, which link it with balconies at either side, permit the entire bridge to be used as a sheltered, open-air terrace in fine summer weather. Doors are aluminum.

The bridge contains dining and living areas, separated by a bar and Hi-Fi cabinet. This space is extended at either end by front and rear entrance halls. Floors (including balconies) are gray-black terrazzo. Insulated, galvanized sheet-metal ducts run beneath the bridge for forced hot-air heating. The basement and retaining walls are reinforced concrete; concrete block is used for crawl spaces and to frame the rest of the house. The exterior walls are finished with integral color stucco. The fireplace and chimney are glazed brick. The vaulted roof has a gold-leaf paper ceiling, aluminum accordion insulation, and copper flashing. Gargoyles by sculptor Robert Engman serve as downspouts over the stream.

1958

Gray House

The steel-frame and curtain-wall structure so familiar to modern office buildings has been delicately scaled down and put to residential use here. Black slate panels form part of the curtain walls, a rather unusual and effective treatment of the material. The resulting floor plan works as efficiently as that of an office and provides a setting more informal, comfortable, and elegant.

Keeping the column-and-beam construction as light as possible, the architects left the steel exposed—but painted it a crisp white to contrast with the exterior walls of black slate, aluminum louvers, and glass panels. By spacing the bays at regular intervals, a flexible pattern of open and closed

interior areas was achieved. Separation of living and sleeping areas, always a major problem in house planning, was effected by centering the kitchen and utilities in a "buffer zone." Inside bathrooms are along a mechanical core.

The rectangular shape of this house was evolved from the simple forms of column-and-beam steel construction. This gives great flexibility to the plan and permits light curtain-wall enclosures. The structural steel frame is frankly expressed and kept as light and delicate as possible to show the strength of the material involved. The curtain-wall panels are of three types: black slate solid panels; double glass set in wood sash and fixed in place; and vent units, with wood doors on the inside, and screens and adjustable aluminum louvers outside.

1958

Starkey House

Lightly poised on tiny steel pins, this house for Mr. and Mrs. Robert J. Starkey hovers quietly over its sloping site to command a panoramic view of Lake Superior. Marcel Breuer combines his typical ingredients of texture, pattern, sun and shadow, and a binuclear plan, to create a design recognizably his, yet aptly suited to its owners and the locale.

On the street front, the house presents a low, conservative facade, with the more spectacular effects reserved for the garden side. The decorative qualities throughout the house are achieved entirely by accenting and contrasting the basic structure and materials. The zoned plan provides one wing for living, dining, kitchen, and utilities—daytime activities and adult entertaining. The second wing houses bedrooms, baths, and a central playroom for the children. Beneath all this are enormous flagstone terraces, sheltered by the house.

The structure of the house is a dramatic factor in its design. Exposed laminated wood columns and girders rest lightly on eight steel pins that extend to bedrock, giving decay and termite protection. Their function is stressed by contrasting the natural wood against the white house sandwiched between. The roof is suspended by steel hangers from the top girders, and surfaced with built-up felt, tar, and gravel.

1958

LOWER LEVEL

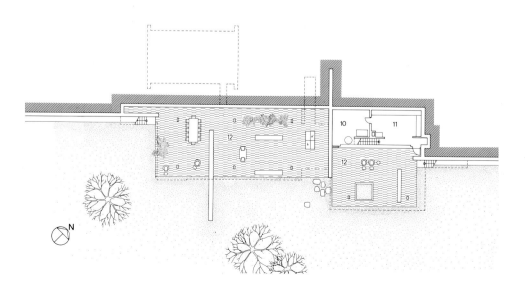

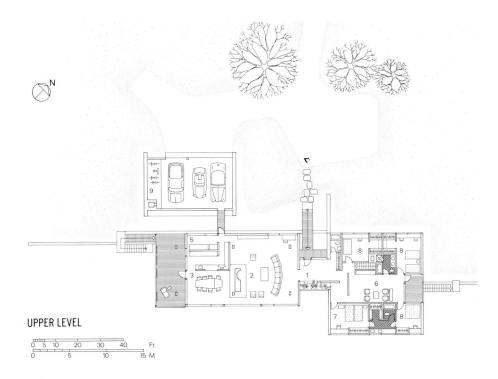

UPPER LEVEL

Sert House

The advance beyond active revolution in architectural design asks much—continuity of discipline, expansion on a principled basis, ability to combine and compose. Thus in days characterized by rampant confusion and fashion one rarely finds an architectural work which is at once as comprehensive and decisive as this house. Such an observation certainly does not indict the profession as a delinquent group. On the other hand, it does suggest there are creative directions other than a subscription to an undisciplined search for novel form and facade.

In view of this it seems to me most significant and gratifying to see José Luis Sert, a leading architect and Dean of the Graduate School of Design, Harvard University, build recently for himself a house that decries fashion and folly in its simplicity, straightforwardness, and respect for time-honored fundamentals. Yet it is without sacrifice of freshness and vitality in the final result—qualities achieved by a balanced concern for the general, the specific, the large, the small, the whole.

The Sert House is built on the patio principle. Situated in a dense urban area, it sensibly extends its encompassing walls to the boundary lines, and puts all its precious ground surface to use, rather than give up some to a no-man's land between itself and an adjacent house; thereby it also

Sert House
Cambridge, Massachusetts
José Luis Sert, Architect
1959

controls its own views. As a type it combines logically in series to create a new streetscape composed solely of patio-enclosing walls, fences, hedges. It allows for a simple, unpretentious life pattern (in spite of society's demands), both in taste and manner. At the same time this system has the inherent advantage of much greater potential for individual owner expression in terms of decoration and facade—style without danger of violent clash between adjacent houses. Swedish Cape Ranches can exist next door to Gas Pipe Moderns without clash, since the street facade conceals all the "wonders" behind.

The architect-owner of the handsome house shown on these pages had for many years been a proponent of the "patio house" as a solution to the problem of the first urban function—the dwelling. His familiar large-scale planning studies for several South American cities propose this house type as a primary dwelling unit of the neighborhood. A neighborhood based on this proposal would consist of houses tightly clustered, each house having access through a patio on one side to a common green network of linear parks linking a series of patio squares. On the opposite side, access would be gained to an entrance patio from an off-street parking area. Streets formed by this arrangement with combinations of patio-enclosing walls, fences, and hedgerows might conceivably have some of the qualities of

a country lane. Our existing urban street pattern provides an unsavory picture in comparison.

It is inevitable that an unequiv-ocal belief such as J. L. Sert's, in the logic of both the "patio house" and its pattern of develop-ment, given due opportunity, would produce a prototype solu-tion. This recently completed house is correctly that.

Situated on a quiet residential street in Cambridge, it is con-structed in ordinary New England fashion, a mixture of brick and wood-stud walls and a wood-joist roof. It does not exert itself struc-turally, does not attempt to use a long-span system in a short-span situation. Neither does it resem-ble its neighbors in exterior form, yet blends into the local scene through its restraint and use of familiar native materials.

Its rather unusual floor plan frankly recognizes the way of life of its inhabitants; this includes frequent large groups in the house-sessions with students and faculty, discussion groups, visit-ing dignitaries, and university parties. Doors and folding parti-tions enable the separation of areas to create privacy and inti-macy, without destroying an essential feeling of openness. Elimination of wasteful and unpleasant corridors is made pos-sible by broadening potential cir-culation spaces into usable areas, i.e., the study (with an excellent architectural and art library) and the dressing room; even the space between the kitchen and the maid's room is a high-content storage area, and the garage is used as a way to a basement workroom (where the paving blocks for the central courtyard were handcast by several enterprising Harvard College students). Primarily an adult house, its yards and encircling character, at the same time, intrigue children.

The landscaped patios provide eventful variety, differing from each other in size, shape, and function. On the west, through the living room the largest patio, paved with cement blocks for outdoor dining, is (otherwise) grassed. The central patio, twenty-four feet square, paved in tiles of gravel set in cement (with the exception of a planting area containing a flowering tree), serves as an extension of the entrance space and living room. On the east, past the study and through a multiuse room, the third, an unpaved cultivated space for sunbathing and gardening, is

enclosed by a Costantino Nivola decorated fence. Generous glass areas, fixed and sliding, open the roofed spaces to those unroofed, framing permanent pictures of sky, treetops, and daily and seasonal change; their careful positioning (and proportioning) allows an uninterrupted view from front fence to rear fence, a total distance of little more than one hundred feet, enabling an enclosure of modest dimension to give the illusion of considerably greater size.

The furnishings are very few—primarily custom-built pieces. Low horizontal living-room seats with brightly colored upholstery—birch-edged panels supported on X-legs; a dining table composed of a slab of glossy black Italian marble carried on steel legs (placed to eliminate conflict with human legs)—its chairs the nine-dollar unfinished department-store variety painted black. In its

simplicity the furniture registers a firm protest to the underthought and overformed nature of much of that currently fashionable.

Fine paintings, including a fifteenth-century Spanish altarpiece, and works of Miró, Léger, and Picasso, are hung, their positions determined in relationship to the architectural surfaces; at night a colorful Miró reflected on the plate glass seems to be suspended in the central patio. Objets d'art are plentiful, representing a multitude of cultures; a collection of gold jewelry (Peruvian, Colombian) meets with the approving eye of a well-designed cat. Against a white background, bright colors appear frequently, especially red and blue. When applied to ventilating panels, window jambs, the fireplace flue, and occurring in the fabrics, they recall the pigments found in the paintings and establish an overall color balance admittedly high in

pitch, in accordance with Mediterranean tradition.

Quickly reviewed in this way, the characteristic elements of the house, general and particular, are found to be simple, logical, unpretentious. The application to each of a uniformly severe critical standard of taste results in a unique and highly personalized composition. The significance, in my opinion, lies in this unified wholeness achieved without superficial theatrics and in the harmonious combination of architecture, landscape, and fine art.

I personally find it to be a warm, alive, refreshing house—one especially pertinent at a time of doubt and indecision.

1959

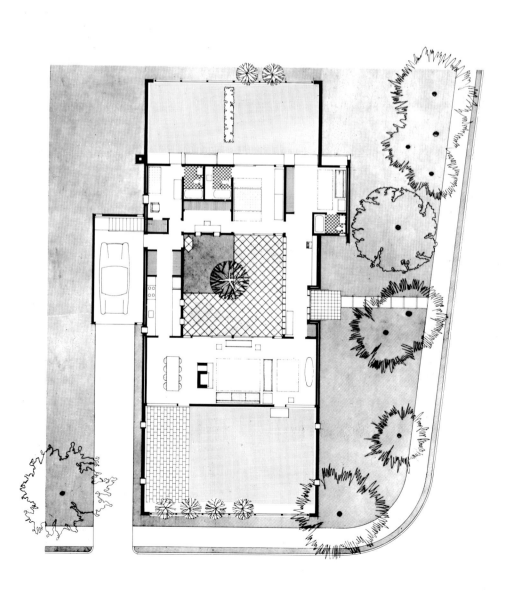

The 1960s

The 1960s: Playing by the Rules

ROBERT CAMPBELL

No decade can be summed up in a sentence. But it's worth trying anyway, as a way of getting a first handle. So here goes: The 1960s, for American architecture, was the decade of trying to figure out how to make beautiful and interesting form without using any ornament.

You couldn't, as an architect, employ ornament because the Modernist Terror was still in full effect. "Ornament is crime," the early modernist Adolf Loos had written. Stick a Greek column or a Palladian window on your house design, and the taste police would put you in jail.

The difficulty was that you and your clients – and the magazines, such as *Record* – were bored silly with endless variations on the simple cubist boxes of modernism. So you had to find some way to enrich your formal vocabulary. But without ornament. That was the Problem of the '60s.

The many solutions the architects found are what we'll be looking at in these *Record* houses of the decade. It's fascinating to consider the houses from this single – admittedly oversimplified – point of view. We see the architects writhing and practically frothing at the mouth in their efforts to burst the straitjacket of the so-called International Style. Some of their inventions look silly in the perspective of time. Others look wonderful. All are responses to the Problem of the '60s.

A few years later, in the '70s, all this came unstuck. Ornament returned. You could enrich your house with all the historical shapes or details you liked. The movement was called postmodernism and it seemed like a release at the time. But in retrospect, it's at least possible to argue that the '60s, struggling for its own kind of freedom within a rigid, unquestioned system of values, was a better era for architecture. Rigid systems have their virtues in the world of art. It's hard to make a great chess move without a board.

There's one other point to be made before we move on to look at the actual houses. It's an obvious one. The '60s was a decade in which many things besides architecture were struggling for freedom. Other values besides those of modernism were under attack. The '50s had been, as much as any decade of this century, an age of consensus. The '60s brought conflict: the civil rights movement, the Vietnam War, the killing of Kennedys and King and Malcolm X, riots in the cities. A new youth culture stuck it to the grown-ups with sex and drugs and rock 'n' roll – and, more relevant, the Free Speech Movement. The architecture of the *Record Houses* traces that historic trajectory. Just as the larger culture moved from the gray flannel suit to the tie-dyed bell-bottom, so architecture moved from the understated black-and-white perfection of an Ezra Stoller photograph to the free colors and shapes of Supergraphics and then postmodernism.

It was, at heart, a trajectory from belief to confusion. The belief – we see it in the early houses – was in the power of professionalism to solve the world's problems. Ten years later, architects had come to think of themselves differently. They became questers, artists, intellectuals, revolutionaries, sociologists, and many other things. But they weren't – at least not in that confident old entitled way – problem solvers. They'd lost the faith.

Robert Venturi's *Complexity and Contradiction in Architecture* nicely marks the fulcrum of the change, coming as it did in 1966, and featuring such antimodern works as Guild House in Philadelphia, with its gold rooftop TV aerial standing in for the ornamental pediments and cupolas of the past. The postmodern love of iconography, its delight in joking and mimicking form for form's sake, was just around the corner – although nobody knew it yet.

The decade thus began with science and ended with art. I remember the beginning very well. I started architecture school in 1963, when Harvard was still giving us – in the first year, especially – the full Bauhaus initiation. Architecture was a cult then. It

OPPOSITE:
FITZPATRICK HOUSE
YORKTOWN, NEW YORK
ROBERT FITZPATRICK, ARCHITECT
1969

PRECEDING PAGES:
BECKWITH HOUSE
FRANKLIN HILLS, MICHIGAN
MEATHE, KESSLER & ASSOCIATES, ARCHITECTS
1961

could behave like a cult because it believed its message. It exploited the same techniques of indoctrination as any other cult – Marines, say, or Maoists. As a student, you were worked around the clock and deprived of sleep. Deadlines were changed unexpectedly. The values you'd grown up with were mocked. You were subjected to intense sessions of group self-criticism (juries, we called them). You were taught a new lingo: A kitchen was a food preparation center, a house was a dwelling unit. The idea was to strip such concepts of the baggage of cultural sentiment, so they could be investigated "objectively."

It was all pseudoscience, based on the fatal misconception that architecture could be nothing *but* problem solving. Understand the problem, we were taught, and the building would design itself. Reading these old texts from *Record* – including the comments of the architects – we often come away with the impression that the site and the program got together and copulated to engender the house. The architect was incidental, a sort of lab technician.

By the time I finished school, in 1967, the university was within a few months of being shut down by a rebellion in which the architecture students took a leading role and for which they designed a classic red-fist poster that instantly went national. If the students were, perhaps, still fodder for cults, the cults in question were certainly not those of architectural modernism.

The decade was too conflicted to give us any masterpiece on the order of Fallingwater or the Gamble House. Maybe there was too strong a sense of belatedness: The "Form-Givers," as Peter Blake called them in his 1960 book *The Master Builders* – Mies van der Rohe, Le Corbusier, and Wright – were of an earlier generation. Perhaps the '60s architects were inhibited by a belief that since form had already been given, it was their fate merely to extend the masters' innovations. But they produced some wonderful works, as this book demonstrates. And what gives these houses their special energy is, it seems to me, precisely the tension – a tension that's almost erotic – between the desire for sensual form and the puritanical modernist ban against it.

Let's take a look. I'd like to begin not at the beginning but with a *Record* House of

1962. The Development House for New Seabury, Cape Cod, by Robert Damora sums up everything they tried to teach me in that first year of architecture school (page 64). It's a splendid house, no question about that. But it's supposed to be so much more than a house. It's supposed to be a prototype: not merely a house, but a whole new rational system for building houses. It is based on an understanding of the manufacturing process that is academic, to say the least. All the magic words are here: everything is modular and interlocking and can be put together or expanded in an endless variety of ways. Hundreds of systems like this were created in those years, when architects were "rethinking" – another buzzword – the way the world was made.

Before the decade ended, the federal government joined the great experiment, funding a program called "Operation Breakthrough," headed by George Romney, a former president of American Motors. Operation Breakthrough was going to find a way to build houses as efficiently as Detroit built cars – an ambition that now inspires amusement, in view of what Japan was about to do to Detroit. And indeed, a different housing system was destined to triumph, one the heavy thinkers didn't even notice was a system. Ordinary studs on sixteen-inch centers, with four-by-eight sheets of plywood and drywall and everything that goes with such elements, turned out to be, in fact, a better and more flexible modular system than anything an architect came up with.

Looking back at it all, I think we can see in the Damora house an exaggeration of the modernist idea that is, already, unmodernist. The house is the fevered postmodern dream of a modernist world: rational, geometric, flexible, and technological to such a pitch that it loses touch with reality and floats across the border of sanity into pure iconography. It's a delightful and self-contained intellectual toy, like a Rubik's Cube. That is its special way of solving the Problem of the '60s.

Ulrich Franzen, in his Essex, Connecticut, house of 1960, finds another way (page 58). He takes the standard glass-walled, flat-roofed box and explodes it. His roof is sucked upward to float like a canopy of leaves. His walls stride forward into the landscape. It's the same trick on which Frank Gehry has based much of his career: For visual interest, pull everything into separate parts. Notice, though, the difference. Franzen is still telling us he's just solving problems. "The plan of the house was devised . . . to simplify living for a family with only part-time commuting help," *Record* informs us. We weep for clients so deprived, but are grateful for the architect who rescued them. "The structure is a carefully engineered steel frame." We recognize the language of pseudoscience. You'd never find anything like it in a magazine today. Notice, too, that Franzen's plan is a "rational" nine-square grid, very much like Damora's.

Marcel Breuer solves the Problem in his own very influential manner. The exteriors of Breuer's houses of this period tend to resemble the shop window of a canny dealer in materials. The house becomes a sampler board of different tones and textures: a little painted stucco, a little stone, a little cedar siding that's maybe horizontal or maybe vertical or maybe even diagonal. Indoors there's perhaps a fabric, selected for texture rather than pattern. Breuer came out of the Bauhaus, with its devotion to the art of collage. He shares with Frank Lloyd Wright a love of natural materials, but much more than Wright he irons his materials into a flat collage. In the Hooper House (page 62), it's mainly the fieldstone we're asked to admire, though there's also bluestone and sisal. The stonework is flattened and exaggerated into something more like a texture than a mass. So treated, it becomes a kind of ornament. We may also notice another *Record* House of this same year, the one by Jules Gregory, which manages to combine Franzen's "Pull It Apart" with Breuer's "Show Them Stone."

Balthazar Korab's wonderful photo of the living room of a 1961 winner presents a different approach (pages 48–9). This is the house as a jewel box. You're supposed to admire the contents, not the container. It's a Cranbrook aesthetic: a family of perfectly positioned, utterly isolated, suavely crafted objects – chairs, lamps, tables, vases – spaced well apart and often turned on the diagonal so they can be appreciated individually. The room is furnished the way you'd set a table. It doesn't need people because it's already inhabited by its elegant things.

Even the fireplace is treated as a freestanding humanoid object. I've never seen a photo that brings back a certain era more intensely.

Another solution to the Problem of the '60s is adopted by several houses. These enliven modernism by marrying it to some regional tradition: the wedding of Local and Global, as we'd put it today, or maybe Venice and the Sea. Robert B. Browne's house (1962) is a good example (page 72). As the editors accurately note, "Modern techniques and materials mingle with tropical romance." The tropical source is the indigenous Caribbean architecture of raised ground floors, deep porches, overhanging shade roofs, and woven sunscreens. Ladd & Kelsey (1962) shotgun a similar marriage in Laguna Beach, this one between modern on the one hand and Californian Let's-Pretend-We're-Spanish patio style on the other. Bennie Gonzales (1967), in Arizona, mates modern with the adobe-brick architecture of the desert. *Record*'s editors cover for Gonzales, lest we imagine he's being nostalgic: "At first glance, this is a very regional Arizona house; but much more important is its expression of the universality and adaptibility of the current contemporary-design idioms." Why more important? We aren't told.

It often happens that architecture, even great architecture, is created in a hopeless attempt to freeze a culture that is disappearing. A minor example is the so-called conversation pit in a *Record* House of 1962. Nothing is clearer today than the fact that conversation – along with other aspects of traditional family and community life – was ebbing fast in the '60s. The conversation pit fetishizes that life, in this house for a childless couple on a lonely site. No doubt the pit has now been converted to an entertainment center: Our friends today enter our homes on screens.

Paul Rudolph's famous Milam House is, for me, the emblem of the decade, just as Rudolph is the emblematic architect (page 76). If ever a designer brought talent and muscle to the Problem of the '60s, it was and still is Rudolph. The result was an increasingly frenzied manipulation of both surface – remember all that corduroy concrete? – and of spatial and sculptural form. Here in this early work, a simple dwelling – an ordinary modern box with an open plan –

FREEMAN RESIDENCE (ATRIUM HOUSE)
GRAND RAPIDS, MICHIGAN
GUNNAR BIRKERTS, ARCHITECT
1968

is made unforgettable by an explosion of entirely superfluous cubist rectangles. As you were required to do in the '60s, Rudolph justifies this baroque extravaganza on functional grounds: It's a sunshade. So why not plant a tree? Two years earlier, a house that didn't make it into *Record* – Robert Venturi's house for his mother – took a different path, seeking form and meaning through memories – however ironic – of the past. A slow starter, the Vanna Venturi House won the race for influence in the end. But neither house is great architecture. Both are too polemical for that.

There isn't enough space to do more than touch on a few more of these extraordinary houses. Craig Ellwood and Gordon Bunshaft and Philip Johnson seek their effects by refining modernism far beyond functionalism into a kind of elegant minimal abstraction. Things are getting pretty ethereal when Ellwood can comment: "Also remarkable is the fact that only two interior partitions touch the exterior wall. The enclosed space therefore 'reads' as a total, and walls 'read' as freestanding planes or volumes within this total." He doesn't bother to cite the 1920s European source for this aesthetic, apparently because he still takes it for granted. Johnson performs an act of modernist revival, building from an early doodle by Mies van der Rohe (House on Lloyd's Neck, page 68). Bunshaft creates the house as art gallery (Bunshaft House, page 84). All three are wonderful. All, in this late gasp of the modern movement, are also extremely self-conscious, and so, one suspects, must be those who live in them.

At the end of the decade we see the emergence of some talents who were to become major figures in the '70s, '80s, and '90s. I. M. Pei, like many of these architects, follows the lead of Le Corbusier, the modernist who first solved the Problem (at Marseilles, Ronchamp, La Tourette, Chandigarh) by turning buildings into massive outdoor sculpture (Slayton Townhouse, page 82). Pei, whose immediate source is Corbu's Maisons Jaoul in Paris (1957), spans thick brick walls with concrete vaults to make an architecture of load and support, an architecture that feels massive and fully built – very different from those airy "planes" and "volumes" of Ellwood's. Later in his career, Pei changed his tune when he began to

base his architecture on an obsession with geometry – arcs, cubes, chords, triangles – some of which he surely gleaned from the work of another important designer of the future, Charles Gwathmey. Richard Meier is a future star too, his Smith House (1968) an unforgettably beautiful icon of the era (page 94). With Meier we've come a long way, from problem solving into pure white abstract form making. You feel you'd have to buy new clothes to enter such perfection without embarrassment.

Charles Moore and partners, by contrast, love everything Meier hates: clutter and comfort and a kind of summer-camp coziness in a house that must contain, somewhere, piles of old *Life* magazines and Monopoly games (Karas House, page 90). The arguments of the '70s are getting under way. Finally, Hugh Newell Jacobsen, in his Trentman House in Washington, D.C., at the very end of the '60s, plays the old game of marrying modern with local, the Georgetown row house in this case (page 98). By so doing he creates the first *Record* House we've seen in a city setting. The honored American houses of the '60s were not concerned with gathering sociably to shape an urban or even suburban Elm Street into a setting for communal life. That's not what they were about. They were about themselves.

So many factors can influence architecture. One of them may have been the simple change, in the architectural press, from black-and-white to color photography. It occurred in the '60s, and no sooner did it happen than the deep-shadowed chiaroscuro of a building like, say, Boston City Hall – so photogenic on Panatomic-X – gave way to the rich Fujichrome colors of postmodernism. Can it be that architects had come to regard the image, rather than the actual house, as the end product of the design process? Was the house now merely a means to the image? It's the image, after all – think of Meier's design, or Rudolph's – that traveled all over the world, pure and uncluttered by the owner's bad housekeeping or ugly furniture, to impress other designers who would never see the original.

Publication and architecture are hopelessly intertwined activities. For that and many other reasons, it's good to have these *Record* houses collected in book form.

JEROME MEIER HOUSE
ESSEX FALLS, NEW JERSEY
RICHARD MEIER, ARCHITECT
1964

House Near Essex, Connecticut

In this remarkable house, architect Franzen develops to a greater degree some of the design hallmarks—for a pavilion house under great soaring roofs—that he started with his own house (see *Record Houses* 1956 [page 22]). In this example, dramatic use was made of a hilltop site to vivify the impression made by the glass pavilion roofed by nine inverted umbrellas, and to exploit to the fullest the surprise of a spectacular view.

The site is a mountaintop with panoramic vistas of the Essex River and its yacht basin, Plum Island, and the Long Island Sound—with occasional glimpses of Montauk light. The vistas are not apparent as one drives up to the mountaintop through a mile of woods.

To heighten the effect, the house was developed with a lower level set into the hillside, retained by walls of granite found on the site. That level contains sleeping and service rooms, as well as the entrance hall; it is a quiet area with closed vistas into the woods and toward a pond. The active areas—living room, dining room, and kitchen—are placed in the open glass pavilion set above the stone podium. As one enters the house, the experience of walking up into the pavilion and the view is one of increasing surprise and excitement.

The plan of the house was devised by Franzen to simplify living for a family with only part-time commuting help. The house is replete with up-to-date equipment and an abundance of built-in storage cabinets. Head-high storage units, finished in walnut or painted white, form the only separation of spaces in the upper living areas; thus the sense of space is increased, and the full impact of the roof structure is felt throughout the area.

The lower level contains bedrooms for the children, flanking a compartmented bath; a master bedroom suite with a little court; and laundry, storage, and utility rooms. The upper level is surrounded by broad decks, and contains a breakfast or hobby area in addition to the living, dining, and kitchen areas.

The master-bedroom suite is designed with provision for a kitchenette, so that it may be used as a self-contained apartment. One of the children's rooms doubles as a guest room; each room has a sliding door for ventilation, and to serve as its own entrance from the outside.

The roof structure is entirely freestanding and self-bracing. It is composed of nine inverted steel-frame umbrellas, which are linked together as three hinged arches. The steel frame is clad in wood, and the ceiling is of treated natural cypress.

The floors of the pavilion are oak blocks, while those of the kitchen and breakfast room are surfaced with vinyl tile. On the lower level, the floor is concrete slab on grade with carpeting in the entrance hall and master bedroom suite. The children's suite has cork floors throughout.

The exterior deck, which surrounds the pavilion on three sides, is of spruce two-by-fours, stained the color of cathedral oak. All trim inside and out is painted a dark plum-brown. Walls on the lower level are plaster or wood paneling. Cost of the house was about twenty dollars per square foot.

1960

Hooper House

Hooper House
Baltimore, Maryland
Marcel Breuer, Architect
Herbert Beckhard, Associate
1960

The forceful simplicity of the Hooper House places it in the proud and solid tradition of many of the great country houses of the past. It is a house that despite an apparent austerity, will age well and acquire more grace and personal atmosphere with use. Its furnishings can be as grand or simple as evolving family tastes indicate. And it contains two of today's greatest luxuries: spaciousness and ease of upkeep.

The scheme is a refinement of some design ideas and trends that have been developing for some time, notably the central-court, binuclear plan. Living, dining, and kitchen areas are on one side of the house, with a playroom (or family room) and seven bedrooms on the other. The playroom serves as an enclosed link between the two elements; in warm weather, it is left open with screen doors at each end.

The site of the Hooper House is a heavily wooded plot that was once a bird sanctuary. The house is placed well back from, and invisible to, the main highway. Its location is on a little bluff overlooking a small lake.

The exterior of the approach, or western facade, of the house is a rugged wall of Maryland fieldstone, broken only for the opening for the entry. This opening is closed by two five-foot-wide sliding glass doors, permitting a view through the entry and court to the lake beyond. The stone facade is an effective barrier to the western sun and helps orient the house to the privacy and view to the east. Other exterior walls are composed of the same stone and sliding glass.

The plan makes use of the drop in the site to provide a lower-level housing for the heating plant, a caretaker's apartment, a garage, and stables. It touches only a corner of the upper floor and extends toward the west along the stone wall defining the upper entrance motor court.

The structure is spanned by steel beams, resting on the stone walls or on Lally columns, and topped with two-by-ten wood joists. Floors are concrete slabs on grade or reinforced concrete where not supported by the ground.

Interior materials include the same stone as the exterior; here they form backgrounds for paintings, tapestries, and sculpture. Other surfaces are gypsum board walls painted gray, acoustical-tile ceilings, and bluestone flooring; bedrooms have cedar walls and vinyl tile or sisal mat floors.

The heating system is a hot-water radiant one, with coils buried in the floor slabs. Baths, kitchen, and playroom have plastic skylights and vent fans. Most lighting is recessed in the ceilings.

The cost of the house excluding lot, landscaping, and furnishings was about $150,000.

1960

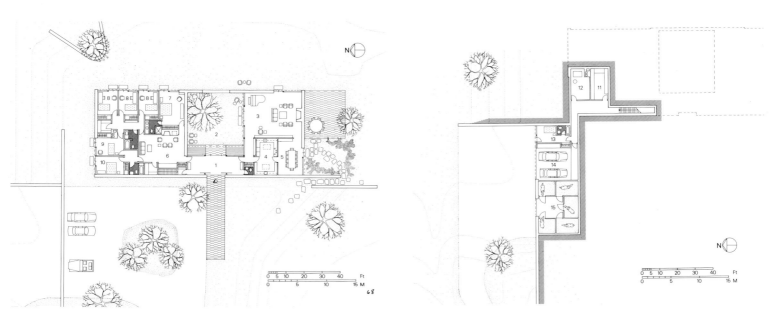

UPPER LEVEL

LOWER LEVEL

Development House for New Seabury

The onus of monotony, a burden of all too many of our large tract house developments, has been vigorously shed in this novel scheme. The architect and builder, working in close cooperation, have devised a moderate-priced house made of a minimum number of prefabricated component parts, which can be speedily put together in an endless variety of ways. No house need be identical to another; each may be adapted to individual requirements of family planning and site topography. Thus, for the projected one-thousand-house development, the effect will be that of homogeneity rather than repetition. Some architectural advice will be available on each house to ensure a good plan arrangement, and to obtain a quality of fresh and spirited design parallel to the pilot model shown in the photographs and drawings on these pages.

Planning for this New Seabury House is based on a grid of sixteen-by-sixteen-foot units. These units interlock into adjacent units in four directions, and may be stacked vertically. Any

number desired may be erected, and in any of a variety of patterns.

Within this structural framework, floors, roofs, and walls may be added or eliminated to achieve a livable complex of enclosed rooms, covered or open courts, and terraces or gardens. A standardized utility core, designed to fit in one of the spaces, contains all mechanical equipment.

The pilot model has five rooms and four terraces set in a pergola of fifteen frame units. In volume production, it is expected to sell for $20,000.

Besides the endless initial arrangements possible with the scheme, it also offers a design that can be easily expanded. By building the entire network of frames at the outset, the house would have an air of size and interest even at its tiny beginning.

The architect of this New Seabury House states that "concrete was used throughout in an effort to utilize the masonry fabrication plants during their slow winter months; the component parts are mass-produced and stockpiled in the winter, and are then available for speedy erection—two to three days—during the rest of the year."

There are six basic structural parts: (1) column or column blocks, (2) beam for floor and roof, (3) floor panel, (4) flat roof panel, (5) folded-plate roof panel, (6) sun or trellis joist. All members are hollow; voids in the floor panels serve as ducts for heating and utilities.

In addition to the panels for floors and roof, rooms are enclosed by a curtain-wall system (used for exterior and interior) assembled from three interlocking component panels: (1) fixed glass panel, (2) fixed sandwich-insulating panel, and (3) operating (sliding) glass or solid panel.

These wall panels connect to the concrete structure through a watertight key-and-slot system. The panels snap in place and, at least in theory, could be quickly removed and snapped back into

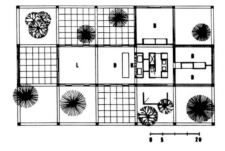

for more costly tile or other super-imposed bathroom waterproofing.

The kitchen opens onto the dining area and is shielded by a work counter/bar; behind this is the heater space; and next is a compartmented bath and two closets opening on the hall.

As the house itself sits on a sort of platform, attractive natural sites can easily be preserved. The pilot model is built with cast columns, but it is projected that mass-produced houses would be constructed with columns made of concrete blocks strung together to give greater flexibility for site adaptation.

Trees and other existing land-scaping can also be easily pre-served as desired with this adaptable house; several such examples can be noted here. In this first house, various levels of terraces and gardens are being developed in the "void" areas of the structural frame grid. It is also projected that a plastic swimming pool will be suspended in one such area.

other sections of the channel frame to create a larger space (which remains unheated) for summer weekend visitors.

Basic to the planning and econ-omy of the New Seabury House is a utility core with all the mechan-ical equipment for the house. The same wall panels are assembled to make walls for the kitchen, the bath, closets, and the heater and utility room. As the panels are waterproof, their use for bath and shower areas eliminates the need

1962

House on Lloyd's Neck

House on Lloyd's Neck
Long Island, New York
Philip Johnson, Architect
1962

The problem of designing a large house for an extremely narrow lot has been solved here by splitting the plan into two pavilions, each offset from the other, with the long axis of each following that of the site. One unit is devoted to living, dining, and the kitchen, with service quarters below; the other contains bedrooms, a library, laundry, and storage. The two units are connected by an interior corridor on the lower level, and by an open terrace above.

The site is one hundred feet above a "fjord" type of inlet and offers very dramatic views. The offset plan of the two pavilions allows views from all rooms—and the major view over the water is capitalized on by the spectacular raised living pavilion shown here. It projects out over the edge of the cliff, giving the effect of being built in the trees, and sheltering a terrace below. The design of this one unit is

UPPER LEVEL

LOWER LEVEL

0   10   20   30   40

based on an early sketch of Mies van der Rohe's, with diagonal trusslike members crossing in front of the glass walls.

The plan of this Long Island house gives excellent separation for living and bedroom areas—an especially useful item for the seaside location where entertaining may be more frequent than in less pleasant locales. The big living area and terraces can accommodate a large number of guests.

The structure is a very nicely proportioned one, with a frame of exposed and painted structural steel on concrete foundations. Exterior walls are of brick and glass; interiors are painted plaster, on wood studs. All ceilings are plaster except for acoustic tile in the playroom. The roof is built-up tar and gravel.

Interiors are simply but well finished. Flooring for the various rooms includes mosaic tile in living areas, rubber tile in the kitchen and the playroom, and ceramic tile in the baths.

1962

Barrows House
Marathon Shores, Key Vaca, Florida
Robert B. Browne, Architect
G. F. Reed, Associate
1962

Barrows House

Modern techniques and materials mingle with tropical romance in the design for this house set on coral rocks jutting into the Atlantic Ocean. The owners, retired after a busy industrial career near Chicago, desired a small, durable home that would provide simple comfort and uncomplicated relaxation. Its otherwise idyllic location posed the big problem of hurricanes.

The result is essentially a large screened porch under a great overhanging metal roof. Rooms are created, for the most part, by folding wood jalousies that can permit complete openness when desired and ventilation control at all times. After the famous Hurricane Donna, the house was undamaged in a town fifty percent leveled.

The plan of the Barrows House gains maximum living area in fine weather by opening all rooms to the screen process.

Plastic storm shutters can be snapped in place for cool or wet spells.

The structure, except for the roof, is all pine and is pressure-treated against insects and mildew. Creosoted posts support floor beams set three-and-one-half feet above grade and two roof beam bands, one at the perimeter and the other inside at the roof break. Floors are two-by-fours spiked solid over the beams. The roof is of two-by-fours on edge, spaced $3^{5/8}$ inches on center, and

covered with a standing-seam membrane of galvanized iron sheet coated with white epoxy.

Equipment includes an oil-fired, forced-air heating system, with glass-fiber ducts under the floor. All closets have dehumidifiers. The kitchen includes built-in range, oven, refrigerator, dishwasher, garbage disposer, and washer-dryer.

1962

Hirsch House

Hirsch House
Highland Park, Illinois
George Fred Keck and William Keck,
Architects
1963

The curving facade of this large, restful house has been well adapted to accommodate several restricting site requirements. The lot is a fair sized, beautifully wooded one on the shore of Lake Michigan. The owners wished to have the house set well back from the street for privacy and to accommodate off-street parking for guests. A large lawn between the house and the lake view was also desired. However, about half of the property consisted of an abrupt slope down to the lake, leaving a not-too-large area for the house and lawn. This was solved nicely by the crescent shape, with ends turning away from the street to encompass a central lawn at the back.

For greater privacy, the front of the house has relatively few openings and mainly contains service areas. All major rooms open on the back to the gallery, lawn, and view.

Parking is provided in a circular entrance drive; at the center is a "drive-through" garage, with doors on both sides, connected to the house by a porte-cochere. The house is black brick with white trim. Windows are fixed glass flanked by louvers, a typical and handsome detail of the Kecks, which can be adjusted for controlled ventilation free from drafts. Screens are fitted over these

ventilators, so the view through any glass is unobstructed.

The Hirsch House was planned for a somewhat formal way of life, and as a suitable background for a growing collection of paintings and sculpture (only a few items from the collection can be noted in these photos). With this in view, rooms are equipped with recessed picture moldings, recessed directional ceiling lights, and (in the living room) stands and glass cases for sculpture.

The structure has poured concrete foundations and a partial basement. The house is air-conditioned and uses gas-fired hot-water heating.

The interior walls are finished with plaster, except for the baths, which are marble and tile. Floors are parquet wood in the living areas, terrazzo in the kitchen, and asphalt tile in the playroom. The kitchen ceiling is acoustical tile to reduce noise transmission. Plastic skylights are used to add

light to the dining room, kitchen, and baths.

The plan is simply organized, with living and dining areas in the center, flanked by bedrooms to the west. The playroom has an area for breakfast and informal meals.

Terraces and walks are slate; there is provision for sculpture to be added outside.

1963

Milam House
St. John's County, Florida
Paul Rudolph, Architect
1963

Milam House

One of the most different designs among this year's *Record* houses, is this one with its very sculptural use of concrete block. The exterior of the house is dominated by the powerful composition of rectangles forming a sunshade across the rear facade. The spirit of this wall is continued on to the interior of the house, where the floors are arranged on seven different levels.

Comments of the owners, after having lived in the house for some time, are worth noting: "We knew enough of Mr. Rudolph's previous works to know that the end result would correspond to our ideas of beauty ... [and] our faith in the architect was well placed. We are extremely fond of the house. Externally, it is a beautiful piece of sculpture—blending graciously with the sea and the sand surrounding it. It is very comforting inside ... different floor levels make it always interesting, always varied."

The house is a very spacious and conveniently arranged one. All the living areas are essentially in one room, with areas for dining, sitting by the fireplace, and the like, created principally by changes in the floor levels. The hallway linking the upstairs bedrooms is treated as a balcony, and adds yet another level to this varied space. As a counterfoil, colors and other decoration are subdued.

As can be noted in these photos of the Milam House, the already big living areas are made to appear even larger and more open by using very few pieces of portable furniture. In fact, about the only ones are the dining table and its seats. Basic seating for conversation and lounging is formed by cushioned units supported by one of the floor levels.

The house is constructed of sand-colored concrete block, left exposed inside and out. The main

UPPER LEVEL

LOWER LEVEL

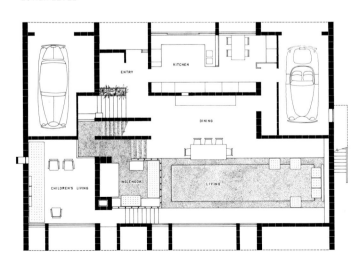

floor is terrazzo, and the upper floors are hardwood or carpet except for tile in the bathrooms. Ceilings are acoustical plaster for noise absorption in the big areas. The small windows in the baths are supplemented for daylighting by plastic skylights. One of the baths also has an outside exit and stair to serve as a dressing area for swimmers from the beach. Bed-room closets are provided in the nooks near each entrance.

The kitchen is conveniently placed for access to the living and dining areas (via a pass-through), to the garage for unloading groceries, and to the front door. The entire house is air-conditioned. The cost of the house itself was $88,074.

1963

Slayton Townhouse

Slayton Townhouse
Washington, D.C.
I. M. Pei & Associates, Architects,
with Kellogg Wong
1964

When Urban Renewal Adminis-
tration Commissioner William
Slayton and his family planned to
return to the city after living in a
suburban home, a search of the
older, built-up neighborhoods of
Washington turned up a bypassed,
vacant lot in the Cleveland Park
area. I. M. Pei's design for the
property has produced a handsome, contemporary version of a
townhouse with a walled-in front
court.

The lot measures 50 by 135 feet,
and has a slight slope away from
the street. This slope was used to
advantage in creating a split-level
scheme well suited to family life
in the city. Great privacy was
achieved not only by the high

wall of the front court, but by almost completely blank walls on the sides—which are quite close to existing houses. Inside, however, the feeling is one of great openness, with front and back walls of glass. The structure is brick bearing wall, topped by a triple, poured concrete vault. The interiors are brick and plaster.

The Slayton House gains a great sense of space and variety by good zoning and its split-level scheme. At the front, the house appears to be a single, high-ceilinged story. The main living areas and adjoin-

ing walled-in garden are on this side. Other rooms, each one bay wide, form a two-story section at the rear. A "service spine" is a buffer between them.

The spatial quality of the vaulted rooms is quite impressive. Mr. Slayton comments: "I remember clearly the day—when it was just becoming twilight—that I drove by the house when the forms for the vaulted roof had been removed. I walked through what is now the glass doors into this space, and for the first time realized what I. M. Pei had conceived.

It was a tremendously moving and emotional experience; I shall never forget it." The vault over the stair is further dramatized by a skylight.

1964

Bunshaft House

Concrete roof beams, travertine-faced concrete, and glass exterior walls with clerestory windows have been used very effectively in this two-bedroom house, which is both a restful weekend retreat for the architect and his wife and an ideal setting for their growing collection. In addition to works by Picasso, Le Corbusier, and Henry Moore, their collection includes some of Mrs. Bunshaft's own work—notably a collection of smiling faces painted on pieces of local stone.

The house fits well into its site, a wooded stretch of land near Georgica Pond at the eastern end of Long Island. As the pond is liable to flood at certain times of the year, the land had to be graded to an elevation of six feet before the house could be erected. The most interesting structural elements are the prestressed concrete T-beams that support the roof and allow space for the installation of a row of clerestory windows in the ends of the channel-shaped sections on either side of the house. As you approach the house, the attractive grille effect of these windows seems to accentuate the pristine simplicity of the travertine-faced concrete walls. A well landscaped drive-way provides the necessary turning space for cars without causing any visual disruption. Floor-to-ceiling glass in the living room opens the house to an expansive view through the trees to the pond.

Too many good private art collections are marred by poor display, or because they conflict with an inappropriate or cluttered home background. The Bunshaft House is, however, a perfect setting for paintings and sculpture and each piece in the collection is seen to its full advantage. Concrete ceilings, white-painted plaster walls and partitions, and

travertine floors reflect the daylight that flows in through glass walls on the southern, western, and eastern exposures, and through the clerestory windows. Most of the furnishings are in shades of white and off-white, but touches of red in rugs and cushions prevent the house from seeming in any way cold or unduly formal.

Despite the dominance of the art, the house has a great deal of character of its own and is much more than just a background for the display of paintings and sculpture. It is very much a com-

fortable and pleasant home and there is no sense of a museum atmosphere.

Views of the Bunshaft House from the outside are quite dramatic, particularly at night, when the effect of artificial light through the clerestory windows can be seen. Wooden screening across the entrance doorway allows one to catch a glimpse of a bold oil painting by Jack Youngerman. The lighting has been carefully planned in relation to the paintings and sculpture.

The living room in the center of the one-hundred-foot-long by

twenty-six-foot-wide house is flanked by the master bedroom to the east and a spare room and a study on the western side. The kitchen is well equipped, and there is plenty of utility and storage space and good circulation.

An effective heating and air-conditioning system makes the house comfortable at all seasons of the year. The changing quality of light and foliage as the year advances are all dramatically reflected on the white interior and exterior surfaces.

1966

Karas House

A three-story-high vertical living space transforms this simple-appearing, shingle-clad house into quarters for a very relaxed way of life. The architects state that "the owners had tired of their large conventional house, and were anxious to spend their limited budget on the excitement usually associated with a vacation house, rather than on the fixtures and appliances ordinarily expected in a house for year-round living." The resulting house thus minimizes "service" aspects (there is a wall-kitchen) and concentrates on a riot of color, space, comfort, books, music. A balcony serves as a quiet sitting nook, and occasionally as a stage for theatricals and a place to hold a band for parties.

The site is also very adaptable to a casual way of life: the land, in a new subdivision in a pine forest,

slopes upward from the street and looks out over Monterey Bay. Windows are carefully placed throughout the house, and at all levels, to overlook the various vistas.

The owners, Mr. and Mrs. Sam Karas, are a couple whose children are almost grown; only one daughter remains at home. Thus "zoning" was not as important as in a house for a larger family; living space, in effect runs throughout the house, wheeling around the little service core on the first floor, and rising to the high shed roof. There are two principal bedrooms and a bath on the second level; on the third level is a loft, reached by a ladder, for visiting children.

Materials throughout the house are simple and easy to keep. The frame is wood studs, joists, and rafters—many of them left exposed. Finished interior walls are redwood plywood (except for plasterboard in the baths).

A "sun scoop" is employed in the Karas House to gain extra light on the pine-forested site, which is often foggy and sunless. Over one of the larger, upper windows in the living space, a "white baffle

Karas House
Monterey, California
MLTW/Moore-Turnbull, Architects
1967

with an enormous yellow sun painted on it is enlisted to bounce south light into the house and to warm up the atmosphere within to a surprising degree," according to the architects.

A lower-ceilinged portion of the first-floor living area is dominated by a large fireplace, which was cast in sand on the floor of the house by the contractor. This area has been treated as a smaller, cozier retreat, as contrasted with the taller reaches of other parts of the room. The furnishings of the house, many of which are built-in, are simple and sturdy and rely for effect on bright splashes of color and a liberal sprinkling of handcrafted accessories. As its original program has intended, the house does lend itself to a sort of perpetual vacation life— and in a remarkable and very different way.

1967

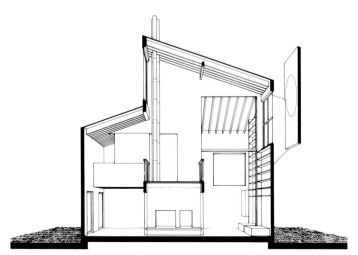

Straus House

*Straus House
Purchase, New York
Gwathmey & Henderson, Architects
1968*

woodland in a manner aimed at creating a series of "visual experiences." They describe it as follows:

Having meandered up the winding drive, catching glimpses through the trees of the house, one arrives in a parking area. With the future addition of a garage and guest house (conceived of as a gate) the scale change from vehicular to pedestrian movement is made specific. From there, a variety of vistas, intensities and directions of light, and changes of shapes and dimensions, hopefully achieve the spatial richness and vitality we desire. Terminating the internal sequence is a complex configuration tying upper living space and stairhall to the anchoring fireplace: here one sees back across the clearing to the enveloping woodland.

1968

Excellent proof that a fresh, visually interesting building can be created within the framework of fairly stringent design codes is furnished by this handsome house. Local ordinances restricted building in the community to two-and-a-half stories in height, with a minimum of thirty-five thousand cubic feet enclosed, and mandatory pitched roofs at not less than 6/12 slope. There were also minimum cost restrictions. Apart from the desire for a strong contemporary design, the owners' requirements were quite simple: living area, dining space, kitchen, and powder room at grade level; three bedrooms and two baths above.

The white-stuccoed, terne-roofed geometric forms that evolved are probably remote from the designs the code-writers envisaged they were espousing, but following them to the letter has produced one of the most creatively significant houses of the year.

The site is a large, wooded one of twenty-five acres. The architects have placed the house in a private clearing within the

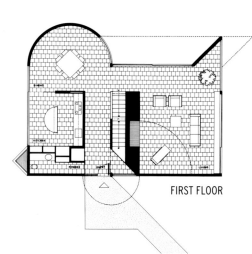

FIRST FLOOR

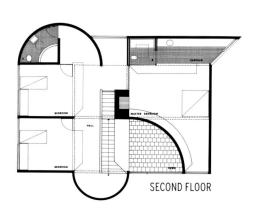

SECOND FLOOR

Smith House

Smith House
Darien, Connecticut
Richard Meier, Architect
1968

Rooms are disposed on three levels, with the "main" floor in the center. The entrance hall, living area, and master-bedroom suite are on this middle level (a slope in the land made possible outside exits on two levels). The top floor contains children's bedrooms, a guest room, and a library/play area—which forms a balcony. The lower level is for dining, kitchen, laundry, and domestic help.

Both the living and the dining areas open directly to outdoor terraces, and the house is topped by an outdoor roof deck. Meier adds that "all the living spaces are interconnected vertically: the living area opening up to the library and down to the dining room. They constitute the open aspect of the house and focus upon the view of the water."

1968

Forceful, direct expression of the plan organization and of the zoning of activities gives this house a freshly handsome, totally unstereotyped character. Thus, the dramatically handled interior spaces are, in projection, used to create an artfully stylized exterior. Design impact is produced by the simplest means, with no frills and a remarkable absence of most current architectural clichés.

Architect Meier states, with equal simplicity:

There is a straightforward use of a wood bearing-wall and framing system for the enclosed half of the building, coordinated with a steel columnar structure for the open living spaces. This allows for a direct expression of the nature of living and service areas with respect to orientation, view, and use. Glass is used extensively in the living areas, while a closed-wall expression is maintained by the use of vertical wood siding for private areas.

The house was designed for a family with two children, and located on a beautiful site of rocky, wooded, irregular terrain overlooking Long Island Sound.

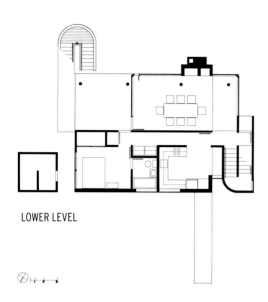

LOWER LEVEL

MIDDLE LEVEL

UPPER LEVEL

Trentman House

Trentman House
Washington, D.C.
Hugh Newell Jacobsen, Architect
1969

Located amid the historic architecture of a quiet, tree-lined Georgetown street, this Washington, D.C., townhouse shows well that residential design can be contemporary and innovative, while respectful of an established neighborhood.

The architect's solution uses timeless materials in their natural state—burgundy-colored brick and gray slate—to keep the texture, scale, and rhythm of the existing street. Materials combine with new interpretation of the traditional arch, bay window, and mansard roof for a forceful design statement, in which the sculptured front bay windows especially are thoroughly modern in their expression of interior space.

Rooms were designed by the architect for a dramatic and uncluttered look usually found in a much larger house. Living room furnishings include silk and molded-plastic or leather-and-chrome chairs. Floors are stained oak. Front rooms—the dining room and kitchen on the second floor and the master bedroom on the third—have a view of a park across the street. Back rooms—second-floor living room and other bedrooms—face a private garden. All are also oriented on two circular stair towers, which form the visual focal points of the house. Each stairwell includes a view through openings, and is capped with a ten-foot plastic dome to bring sunlight down throughout the house. White walls and designed lighting add to the expansive quality of the scheme, which packs a great deal of comfort into an urban lot, thus offering its owners many qualities of a detached, suburban house with the many advantages of urban living.

The traditional townhouse, which fulfills a contemporary need, has, in this very spirited design, found a thoroughly contemporary expression.

1969

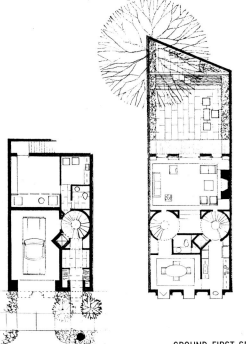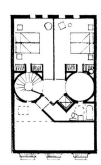

GROUND, FIRST, SECOND, AND THIRD LEVELS

The 1970s

PRECEDING PAGES:
BINKER BARN
SEA RANCH, CALIFORNIA
MLTW/MOORE-TURNBULL, ARCHITECTS
1973

APARTMENTS
TUSTIN, CALIFORNIA
BACKEN, ARRIGONI & ROSS, ARCHITECTS
1973

The 1970s: A Time of Upheaval

Even as the 1970s began, the 1960s were far from over. Nineteen seventy was the year of the ill-fated student uprising at Kent State, the vigilant women's rights march down Fifth Avenue in New York, and the first national observance of the environmentally conscious Earth Day.

As the 1970s progressed, Vietnam peace marches, already a common occurrence of the 1960s, grew in size, until the United States finally signed the Paris Peace Treaty in 1973 and fled Indochina completely in 1975. By then, however, the Watergate scandal had emerged as another governmental embarassment, forcing President Nixon's resignation in 1974. On top of that, a recession of unexpected force hit Americans used to the boom years of the 1950s and '60s. Gas shortages and dramatic price hikes followed the rise to international power of the Organization of Petroleum Exporting Countries. And the Middle East became the next arena for international strife.

This context is interesting, and perhaps instructive, because it sheds light on some of the architectural developments of the 1970s as illustrated in the pages of *Record Houses*. A correlation between the events, the shifting values of the times, and their expression in architectural design is not often easy to detect. If certain architects in the 1970s, particularly the younger ones, identified with the counterculture, their inclinations were not quickly registered on the design of the single-family house for (usually) affluent clients.

Nevertheless, a seriously antiestablishment "revolution" was taking place among the younger members of the architectural profession. Provoked at first by Robert Venturi's writings and work in the 1960s, a "return to historicism" gradually made itself felt as a challenge to modernist architecture's hegemony in postwar America. Venturi, his partner, Denise Scott Brown, plus Charles Moore, Michael Graves, Robert A. M. Stern, and Stanley Tigerman, to name just a few of the more visible examples, were all

pursuing various ways of unmooring architecture from its modernist anchor. The house was the laboratory for their postmodern ideas. Yet very few of their houses, with the exception of those by Charles Moore, would be published in *Record* in this particular decade. Even the most modernist of the avant-garde architects of this generation, such as Peter Eisenman or Frank Gehry, were to publish elsewhere during this period. The absence of this avant-garde was probably not an oversight and had to do with the particular vision of the editors of *Record* at that time.

The editors, as evidenced by the selection in *Record Houses* during these years, seemed rather suspicious of up-to-the-minute, highly charged responses to the changing social, cultural, or architectural pulse of the times. Instead, they were more oriented to spotlighting architecture they felt had a timeless quality to it — a quality they saw most evidently embodied by modernist architecture.

Therefore, much of the architecture shown in *Record Houses* in the 1970s adhered to modernist principles that had been developing in the United States throughout the twentieth century, and especially in the decades since World War II. These included a strong value placed on simple, functional planning, the straightforward expression of structure, and the integration of indoor with outdoor spaces. It also meant the employment of the latest technologies in building construction. Applied ornament was naturally eschewed, since beauty was a by-product resulting from good planning and logical building.

Nevertheless, it should be argued, certain architectural tendencies, manifested in *Record Houses* in the 1970s, were prompted or at least reinforced by sociocultural concerns of the time. In particular, the commitment to building with natural materials and with indigenous construction methods, conserving energy use, and preserving old structures, was to receive added impetus in

PRIVATE RESIDENCE
DARIEN, CONNECTICUT
HUYGENS AND TAPPÉ INC. (NOW
DIMELLA SHAFFER ASSOCIATES),
ARCHITECTS
1974

the decade. Yet in its overall design direction, *Record Houses* continued – as it had since its inception in the 1950s – to document the intense effect on postwar architecture of Walter Gropius, Frank Lloyd Wright, Le Corbusier, and Mies van der Rohe. The way this influence operated could be seen particularly in the case of Walter Gropius, who had come to Harvard's Graduate School of Design in 1937. There he taught future major architects, such as Edward Larrabee Barnes, Philip Johnson, I. M. Pei, Paul Rudolph, Ulrich Franzen, John Johansen, Harry Cobb, and others.

By the 1970s this generation of Harvard-trained architects formed a significant part of the mainstream of architectural practice. While most of the architects had by then attained fame for their office and apartment towers, museums, cultural centers, institutions, and schools, in many cases they continued to design houses either for themselves or for special clients. Earlier in their careers, they had accepted residential commissions because that was all they could command. Now they took on the design of houses mainly to explore and refine ideas that could be applied in their larger projects.

For this reason, it is not surprising to find Edward Larrabee Barnes's design for a house on Mount Desert Island in Maine, published in *Record Houses* in 1976, to be one of his most accomplished works of this era (Heckscher House, page 124). Even though he already had completed high-profile projects, such as the Walker Art Center in Minneapolis (1974), and would soon embark on the design of the IBM Tower in New York City (completed in 1983), he turned his attention to the vacation house. The clean, angular forms with knife-edge silhouettes, shingle cladding, and steeply pitched roofs of the Maine house were very much Barnes's style. A serene grouping of discrete pavilions placed around an outdoor deck evoked the vernacular of Maine fishing villages, while the open volumes and interpenetration of interior and outdoor spaces adhered to principles of modernism.

Another Gropius-trained architect, Paul Rudolph, used a different variation of modernist principles with a steel-and-glass townhouse he designed in Manhattan (Hirsch/Halston Townhouse, page 112). Although Rudolph has designed houses

throughout his career, he was also involved in the 1960s and '70s in such large-scale projects as the Burroughs-Wellcome offices in Durham, North Carolina, finished in 1969. The New York townhouse, a dark glass and steel-frame structure, was discreetly wedged between older townhouses on a tree-lined residential street on the Upper East Side. Yet on the inside, the house quickly assumed another architectural persona. Here the interior opened up dramatically to a triple-height living room topped by a skylight, with a large glass wall at the rear enclosing a small greenhouse. The house, purchased shortly after completion by the fashion designer Halston, attested to the fact that a modern house could adapt well to a traditional context.

If Gropius and other Bauhaus architects, such as Marcel Breuer or Mies van der Rohe, had figured significantly in bringing modern design to America during the 1940s and '50s, Frank Lloyd Wright's imprint on domestic architecture in the United States was no less felt. By the 1970s, the natural basis for building that Wright had so long argued for seemed even more relevant, as the cultural climate became attuned to issues of environmental awareness.

Indeed, in 1978, a *Record* House in central Arkansas designed by E. Fay Jones showed Wrightian principles to be viable almost eight decades after Wright began developing them (page 150). The long, low-slung lines of Jones's house, with its sheltering wood-shingled roofs, its deeply cantilevered overhangs, and its cruciform plan, were typical of Wright's Prairie Style houses. Along with the spatial richness of the interior, it signaled Wright's enduring impact on those who, like Jones, studied with the master at Taliesin before going out on their own.

In spite of some efforts to make architecture more responsive to indigenous materials and methods of construction, a very different variant of modernist architecture also thrived in the 1970s. "High-tech" architecture was to receive a strong boost by the opening of the Centre Pompidou in Paris in 1977. Designed by Richard Rogers and Renzo Piano, the building emphatically reasserted modernist architecture's premise that design should be based on advanced technology. During the time it was being constructed, a number of architects in England, Europe, and North America, also attracted to this vocabulary, set out to prove that these materials and technologies were appropriate even for residential work. The Wolf House, designed by Barton Myers in Toronto, and published in *Record Houses* in 1977, illustrated quite convincingly that steel columns, metal decking, and open-web-joist construction offered a delicacy desirable at a domestic scale (page 126). Another house, by Bohlin and Powell in West Cornwall, Connecticut, showed a proclivity for industrial building techniques combined with an affinity to nature (page 120). The house integrates into a singular entity both cedar siding, which was stained green to blend with the forest setting, and technically oriented elements – specifically large expanses of industrial-type windows.

By the 1970s, many of the kinks had been ironed out of earlier experimental, modernist designs. Problems of planning for a typical family had been solved. New building techniques had been corrected so that, for example, flat roofs and large expanses of glass didn't leak (well, not usually). Certain other architectural elements, aesthetic ones at that, could be seen creeping back into the work of modernists. These architects were trained, as Klaus Herdeg points out in *The Decorated Diagram: Harvard Architecture and the Failure of the Bauhaus Legacy* (1983), to have "an almost reflex mistrust of architecture as art."

This "creeping back" of aesthetics into modernist architecture often assumed, as Herdeg notes, a "formalist" dimension. Formalism, in modernist terms, usually implies a particularly strong sculptural emphasis on interlocking geometries of plan, section, and elevation. While formalistic architecture has been criticized for ignoring other concerns, such as context or function, it can result in eye-catching, if hard-to-live-in, spaces.

Norman Jaffe, a New York architect who achieved a certain renown for his houses on Long Island, created extravagantly geometrical designs that more or less elaborated some of the directions Barnes and Rudolph had explored before him. His dramatic, soaring volumes and silhouettes that pierced the sky lacked the conceptual rigor of his precedessors, but made up for this with an exuberance that proved seductive

GRAHAM HOUSE
FAIRFIELD, CONNECTICUT
ELIOT NOYES, ARCHITECT
1971

to his clients. A house he designed in eastern Long Island, published in 1977, uses cedar shingles, a material popular on the East Coast for cladding walls and roofs, in order to make a highly sculptural, visible statement about man's fight to stay on top of nature, literally and symbolically (Krieger House, page 140).

Some of the more arresting gestures of the modernist age that could also be called formalist depended less on the triangles, cubes, squares, or rectangles of a geometrically obsessed formalism, than on organic amoebalike shapes. For example, the voluptuousness of John Lautner's architecture combined with his splashy sense of technical daring to give his work a distinct imprimatur. Like many of his houses in and around Los Angeles, where he had his office, Lautner's Arango House in Acapulco, Mexico, published in *Record* in 1977, dashingly displays free-flowing forms not constrained by the Bauhaus ethic (page 134). Curving walls, bedrooms that are pie-shaped, a living room reached by a bridge over a stream, and a canopylike concrete roof convey not only an attachment to the world of tomorrow, but also visionary building techniques that were spawned by modernist principles.

A younger generation of architects who had begun their architectural practices in the 1960s showed more sympathy with the architecture of Le Corbusier than with that of other modernist pioneers, such as Gropius, Wright, or Mies van der Rohe. For example, Richard Meier drew upon the vocabulary and spatial implications of Le Corbusier's architecture in a private residence in Westchester, New York, published in *Record Houses* in 1977 (Shamberg House, page 130). Meier elaborated and refined Corbu's own tight, cubic volumes, establishing within them a contrapuntal play of curved elements such as stairs, mezzanines, fireplaces, and protruding balconies.

Similarly, a house by Gwathmey, Henderson and Siegel, published in *Record* in 1970, demonstrated an affinity to Corbusian motifs (page 1). In this case, Charles Gwathmey and his partners emphasized the use of natural wood instead of white stucco and introduced robust, cylindrical and circular segmented forms against rectilinear volumes. This formalism is such that "[o]ne finds almost no gratuitous moves, almost nothing that isn't motivated to generate a specific experience," notes Peggy Deamer in an article about Gwathmey in *ANY* magazine in 1995.

Le Corbusier's oeuvre clearly provided a rich vocabulary, which architects even younger than Meier and Gwathmey continued to mine during the 1970s. Some, like Anthony Ames, with his Hulse House (1978) in Atlanta, stayed within a simplified rendition of a Meier riff on Le Corbusier (page 144). Others pursued a more elaborate trajectory, such as Alan Chimacoff and Steven Peterson with their design for the Lowenstein House (1973) in Montauk, Long Island. Using painted plywood and wood-frame construction, they were concerned with the layering of spaces and various forms of transparency possible in architectural form.

Regional variations on the modernist vocabulary in response to particular climates and local building materials are nothing new to modern house design. The wood-and-stone houses of Gropius and Breuer on the East Coast, and the "Bay Region style" houses of William Wurster and others on the West Coast, not to mention Frank Lloyd Wright's Prairie Style and Usonian houses in the Midwest and elsewhere, attest to the success with which modern architecture could be accommodated to a particular region. The value of working with natural materials and standard techniques of constuction had always been acknowledged by architects who found that newly industrialized materials and construction techniques could be costly and impractical. Nevertheless, in the 1970s the value of designing according to regional techniques and materials became even more pronounced. Not only did the growth of a counterculture and environmentalism increase the receptiveness to traditional building forms and methods, but the oil price increases from OPEC meant that heating or cooling a modernist house could be prohibitive. The expanses of glass and other materials that were inefficient in holding the heat in cold weather, or providing natural means of cooling and ventilation in warm weather, were indeed a problem.

Antoine Predock, an architect based in Albuquerque, New Mexico, has long been identified with using indigenous building

WIERDSMA HOUSE
NANTUCKET, MASSACHUSETTS
LOUIS MACKALL, ARCHITECT
1976

techniques and materials. In his La Luz Townhouses published in *Record Houses* in 1970 (page 116), the massive adobe walls of the low-rise apartments follow time-honored methods for holding heat in the day, which is then released at night. Glass windows are set deeply within the volume of the building to provide natural light. Cross-ventilation is also a factor in positioning the apartments on the sloping site. Later in the decade, a private house designed by Predock, published in 1977, featured solar collectors placed on a shed roof (House in the Sandia Mountains, page 142). In this move to a more active solar heating, the collectors heated water, which was then used to warm the house and the pool.

The interest in architecture indigenous to the nation's different geographic regions continued to deepen throughout this decade. Already in 1964, the Sea Ranch compound in northern California, designed by MLTW Associates (Moore Lyndon Turnbull Whitaker), had established a model of a modernist vocabulary melded with a regional farmhouse vernacular. As shown by a vacation house in *Record Houses* 1973 (pages 100–01), designed by MLTW/Moore-Turnbull, the rough exterior wood cladding, gable roofs, and soaring barnlike interior spaces of the older anonymous architectural tradition could be combined effectively with the expansive fenestration and efficient planning of modern spaces.

In the 1960s a grassroots movement of laypeople as well as architects gradually gained power in preserving landmark structures. Inflamed by the growing sense of loss over popular older buildings that had been torn down, often to make way for new modern ones, the movement broadened in the 1970s to include the protection of whole communities. The increased veneration of historic American architecture went hand in hand with rehabilitating urban cores, fixing up the "Main Streets" of towns, and converting older industrial buildings to new uses. When an economic recession hit the United States in the early to mid-1970s, warehouses and loft buildings, as well as barns, were deemed all the more desirable for this kind of recycling.

In the case of a barn renovated for a house on the Eastern Shore of Maryland, published in the 1978 issue of *Record Houses*,

Moore Grover Harper, Charles Moore's firm in Essex, Connecticut, retained the barn's mid-nineteenth-century stone base (Barn on the Choptank, page 148). They built the new structure above it, exposing the timber framing in the old manner. By including solar collectors as well, the architects created a new "modern" house that very much reflected the spirit of the times.

Like Moore and his colleagues, a number of architects became more and more fascinated with incorporating traditional architectural vocabulary in their new designs. For example, Huygens and Tappé's house in Darien, Connecticut, published in 1974, has strong historicist overtones (page 104). The L-shaped house features the broad and deep hipped roofs, overhanging eaves, and large chimneys evocative of late-nineteenth-century and early-twentieth-century architects such as C. F. A. Voysey or Gunnar Asplund.

In general, however, as noted above, the postmodernist investigations into an architecture with "meaning," or an architecture that communicated to the public about history and context, were left for other audiences, and other publications. Postmodern architects often condemned the pitfalls of modernism's success, in which knockoffs and misapplied ideas banalized the substance and intent of the principles. They couldn't avoid, however, the same commercialization of their own designs, either by their imitators – or by themselves. Some of their thinking withstood the test of time according to *Record Houses*'s standards, and eventually the work appeared in its pages. Some, but not all.

Meanwhile, the social and intellectual currents, so identifiable at the beginning of the decade, would gradually be transformed in the 1970s. In time, they would affect the generation entering architectural practice in the 1980s in unpredictable ways. A stagnant economy combined with high inflation took hold of America, as other nations began to lead the world in economic growth. America's young adults, once raised on the Protestant ethic of working hard now and saving for tomorrow, began to jettison such value systems. As Christopher Lasch wrote in *The Culture of Narcissism: American Life in an Age of Diminishing Expectations*, published in 1979, "a new ethic of self-

preservation" had seized the day. Living for the present seemed to be a more viable way of approaching the uncertain future. Architecture found itself in a quandary. "Timeless" architecture was being redefined at the beginning of the 1980s by a new and experimental approach to design that consciously incorporated historical elements into its language of form. What had previously appeared to be timeless in modernism – as illustrated by the *Record* houses of the 1970s – seemed to some to be dated. Yet that too would change.

COHEN HOUSE
SOUTH ORANGE, NEW JERSEY
BREUER AND BECKHARD, ARCHITECTS
1978

Hirsch/Halston Townhouse

Paul Rudolph has introduced a number of spatial and planning innovations and surprises into his design for this New York townhouse. Behind an elegantly disciplined and somewhat sober facade (brown-painted steel set with obscure, brown, structural glass panels), one enters into a skillfully lighted, white-gray-black series of spaces that culminate in a big, twenty-seven-foot-high living area backed by a three-story greenhouse. Level changes, balconies, open stairs, and tidily integrated fittings abound, in Rudolph's typical fashion, to create a lot of variety and interest in a very cohesive series of spaces.

The house was built on the existing frame of an 1860 coach house, which originally had three floors. A fourth level was achieved in the new house, and within the original space, by creating a mezzanine for the master bedroom suite and its adjoining sitting-room balcony.

The usual back garden—one of the the great pleasures in a townhouse—has been raised to the top level; greenery and a great sense of openness have been introduced into the living area by skylights and the tall greenhouse. Mirrored walls line the lower portions of the greenhouse to augment the effect and the apparent depth. A balcony/bedroom (which can be closed by folding panels) also overlooks the greenhouse, and is connected by a bridge to the game-room level. An open stair connects the living area with the master bedroom suite, and an elevator and a central stair connect all levels.

Floors on the entire first level are surfaced with black slate, and the slate is continued around the dropped living-room area as a sill for sitting or counter space.

1970

GROUND LEVEL

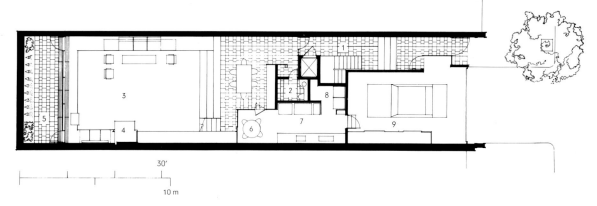

30'

10 m

MEZZANINE

UPPER LEVEL

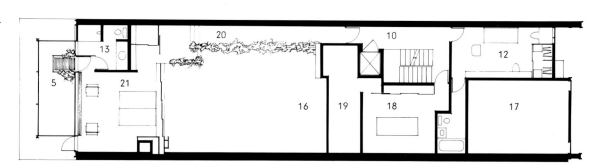

PENTHOUSE

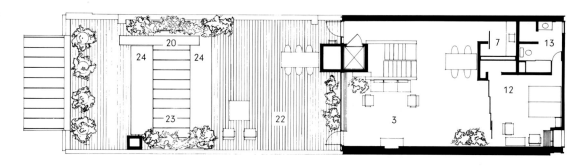

La Luz Townhouses

*La Luz Townhouses
Albuquerque, New Mexico
Antoine Predock, Architect
1970*

There is a rare kind of appropriateness to this cluster of townhouses— built in the early stages of what will be a five-hundred-acre community just outside Albuquerque. Most obviously, the clustering, the use of adobe, and some of the forms are traditional. But where tradition is called on, it is called on for the way it works and not the way it looks.

The massive adobe walls serve as heat reservoirs—blocking heat

during the day and releasing it at night; the walls are essentially blank on the western wall, but open wide on the east to the views down the semiarid mesa to the contrasting green band along the Rio Grande.

The major glass areas are set back beneath deep concrete fascias; and even small windows are set deep in recesses in the walls. To add light without heat or glare, some walls are stuccoed white to bounce light into a room.

Not just the sun, but the wind, is a major factor in the design. High walls protect yards and patios from the wind; but cross ventilation in summer is assured by the placement of the buildings on the slope. In contrast, the often strong and dust-laden spring wind, typically from the west, is blocked by the closed walls of the complex. And perhaps equally essential, at least psychologically in this dry area, are the fountains in the patio areas.

As the plan shows, the major living spaces—with their changes of level and wall plane—all open wide to the view and the breeze; the neatly zoned bedroom area is, appropriately, more sheltered. Because of the changes in the site contours, the interior spaces of the units are pleasantly varied.

1970

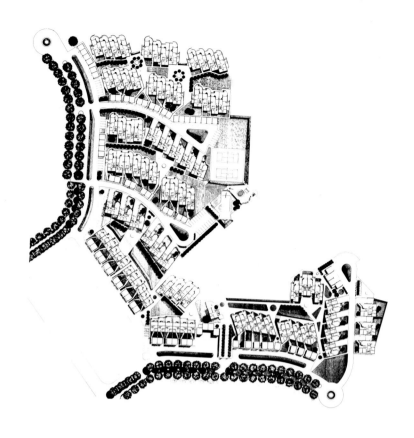

Connecticut House

*Connecticut House
West Cornwall, Connecticut
Bohlin and Powell, Architects
1976*

Its cedar siding stained green to blend with the leaves of a surrounding forest, this house—designed by architect Peter Bohlin for his parents—is in fine sympathy with a natural site of eighteen acres in West Cornwall, Connecticut. Seemingly modest from the approach, the building is actually a carefully studied progression of vertically expanding spaces, which lead the visitor from the dark shade of evergreen trees at the drive and entry bridge into

the high living room with a view of dappled sunlight through lacy deciduous branches.

An industrial-type light standard on the parking-lot side of the bridge begins a series of vertical, rust-red-painted orientation points in the visitor's progress. Others are the surrounds of the glazed front door, those round exposed-concrete columns that extend through the interior, and—finally—the industrial-type framing of the living room

windows exposing the climactic view. The route over the bridge leads past the end of the building, which is only twelve feet wide, under the low roof of the porch, and down several flights of stairs until the full height of the living room is reached.

Careful attention to detail has made a dramatic product of simple materials, such as corrugated aluminum for roofing, tongue-and-groove siding, and circular concrete piers. Bohlin states that

the contrast between large sheets of glass in the standard, black-finished sliding doors and the small panes of glass elsewhere (also standard) is intentional.

Costs for the eighteen-hundred-square-foot structure were just over thirty dollars per foot. The project has won two awards for design.

1976

Heckscher House

Woven into a spruce grove on the
Maine coast, this beautifully
restrained vacation house was
built for a man who is an
author/scholar, interested in public service. Among his wife's varied interests are calligraphy and
cooking. Their children are
grown and living away but often
visit, bringing family or friends
when they do. The program,
therefore, suggested flexibility.
The site suggested modesty.

Barnes began by developing
four separate structures: a studio
tower with laundry below; a one-
bedroom house with living, dining, and kitchen; a two-story
guest house; and a high-ceilinged

library/study. Each of the elements is shaped in simple, vernacular forms finished in wood shingle, each is artfully placed in relation to the others, and all are spun together by a rambling wood deck that opens at intervals to arresting coastal views. The whole composition keeps a respectful distance from the shoreline.

The detailing throughout the house is spare and elegant in its simplicity. The roof planes turn down into the wall planes, for instance, without the interruption of bargeboard or fascia. Trim around openings is so reticent it all but disappears. At one corner of the deck, however, just off the kitchen, the need for a shaded outdoor eating area produced a novel and pleasantly flamboyant series of details. The architect set a spinnaker on booms—a sail that can be adjusted to a range of sun angles by hand-operated winches mounted on the deck.

Though elegant in its details, the house has some of the same hardy character and stern New England virtues that we associate with the Maine fishing villages its massing seems to reflect. No roofs connect its four units and the access road stops two hundred feet short of the house.

1976

Wolf House

There have been earlier attempts (few as successful) in Canada, the United States, and elsewhere to blur the distinction between industrial and residential design vocabularies. Perhaps it was always a needless distinction, but it is still stimulating to see the steel columns, the metal deck, and the delicate tracery of open web joists transfer their precise elegance from factory to home so easily and persuasively.

Inside the basic framework that these elements create is a secondary level of modification and texturing. It includes sculptured ductwork that traces powerful linear patterns throughout the house. It includes drop screens that temper the daylight at outside walls or skylights. And it also includes the entirely appropriate use of unexpected hardware and fixtures that are always within the residential designer's reach but seldom find their way into his specifications. It is a beautifully conceived house, and even those whose cup of tea it is not will find much to linger over in its use of materials and its details.

The plan of the Wolf House is deceptively simple. It is a two-

story, rectangular volume with a bite out of the center of one of its long sides—a bite that admits light and offers views from the normally "dead" waist section of such plans.

The house is lifted above the site to minimize the foundation problems that might otherwise have developed on twenty feet of new fill over a subterranean stream. The upper level contains bedrooms, baths, a play area, and a study. Below, the principal spaces are arranged to take advantage of views to the park at the west. The closed side of the house, clad in aluminum siding, faces neighbors to the east.

In its rhythms, its textures, and handing of its details, the Wolf residence is beautifully organized and very skillfully executed.

1977

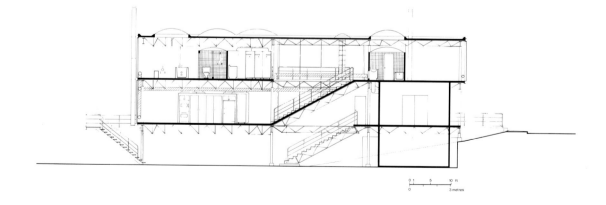

Shamberg House

The owners already had a small and no-longer-adequate house on this property when they commissioned Richard Meier to help them examine their building options. After study, the decision was taken to treat the new structure as freestanding and self-sufficient, but to retain the existing structure as a pool house and guest annex.

As privacy requirements on this thickly treed site were scant, Meier strove to make the new house as open as possible. The entry is on the uphill side across a narrow, playfully detailed bridge. From this arrival point, overlooking the main living spaces, the entire interior volume is revealed—as is the relationship between the house and its sloping site. The Meier design idiom—the white planar surfaces, the exquisite pipe rail sculptures, the absolutely minimal detail—are all here in their now familiar forms but with at least one important variation. In this house, the architect has introduced a series

Shamberg House
Westchester, New York
Richard Meier & Associates,
Architects
1977

of gently baroque curves that play against the otherwise severe rectilinear geometry with much more than mere esoteric effect. The deck, extending the master bedroom to the outside, is one such curve. The imprint on the fireplace breast is another. The main stair, leading from the entry landing to the living room, is a third. The stair's gentle curve carries the visitor around a protruding pipe column, heightening its presence, and putting visual pressure on the living-room space. The flow of space through the rest of the house is almost uninter-rupted except that the upstairs study is kept rather private.

This house makes a family with the Smith, Weinstein, and Douglas houses, all published previously in *Architectural Record* between 1969 and the present. To Meier, they represent a completed body of work, a theme with variations extended and examined rather fully.

Any new houses, says Meier, will explore some new themes.

1977

FIRST FLOOR

SECOND FLOOR

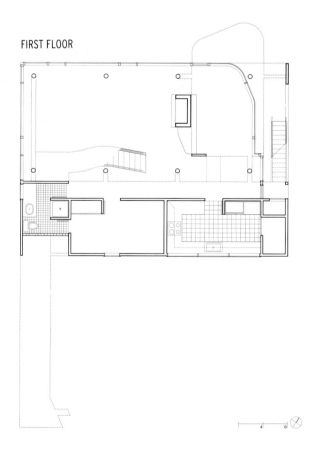

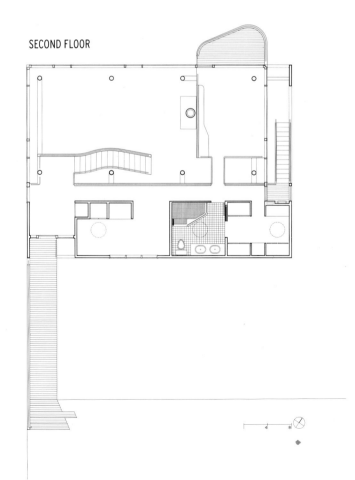

Arango House

Arango House
Acapulco, Mexico
John Lautner, Architect
1977

The effect of this weekend and vacation house, hugging a mountainside above Acapulco Bay, is about as mesmerizing as the margaritas you had better not have too many of if you plan to stroll around its cantilevered terrace.

Though casually lived in, the architecture was in no sense casually concocted, as many dwellings in these parts are, to resemble

haciendas, missions, or stage sets for Zorro. This concrete structure, with floors of marble, requires little maintenance. An organic element of its natural and cultural setting, it gathers the bay into an embrace that is as exciting as its relationship to the terrain.

You curl down a gently sloped driveway from the hill above. Boulders, flowers, and trees edge

the entry beneath a colossal concrete sombrero of a roof, and this covers *everything*, meaning a vast living area terrace that is reached, from the entrance area, by a little bridge. It spans a six-foot-wide pool, a "stream" really, which runs all the way around the perimeter of the area. Looking out, the water of the bay below and the water of the pool blend

together. So visually and psychologically, you seem to be suspended between sea and sky. The plan was shaped to crop out foreground views on down the mountainside, and with the aqueous metaphor of its curving edge, the space, served up as if on a sumptuous tray, plays on the affinity you feel with nature.

Glassed-in and louvered-in, the lower-level bedrooms—of which there are five for the family, another for guests, and three more for servants—open onto quiet terraces or, oppositely, out to the bay. Just down a bit, reached by jutting, angular stairs, is another pool for more strenuous strokes. The whole place is good exercise, especially for the senses, and you're drinking to it.

1977

LOWER LEVEL

UPPER LEVEL

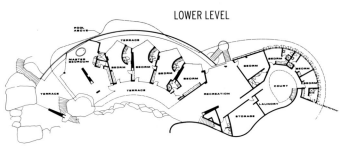
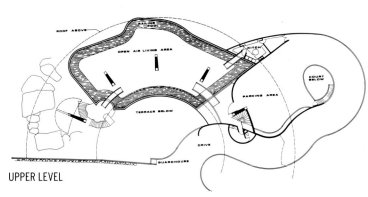

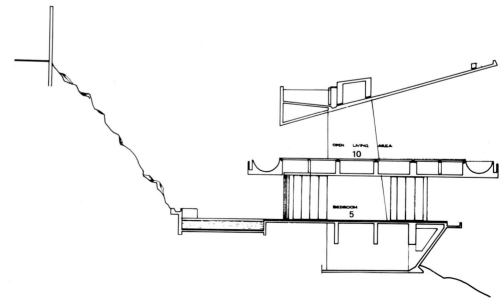

Krieger House

Perhaps at first it seems to strain for effect. Perhaps its geometry seems unnecessarily complex and its spatial development too elaborate for a simple weekend house overlooking the Atlantic. But look closely at the plan these forms enclose. The plan is real. The plan is problems solved.

There is a clear hierarchy of spaces and their relationships are logically ordered. All the spaces but two small guest rooms are gathered under one powerful roof form, and the top of the stair is the point of intersection for all the major planes and spaces. And

from this point, the really splendid ocean view is fully revealed for the first time. Living room, dining space, kitchen, and master bedroom above exploit this view fully, as does the elevated deck that thrusts out from the living/dining space over the lip of the dune in the direction of the ocean. From each of these spaces, the view extends outward all the way to the horizon.

The use of a single exterior finish—cedar shingle—is eminently sensible on a site so exposed to the corrosive action of salt, of wind, of wind-driven rain. And in addition the unity of surface it achieves is important in so complex a form where the classic distinction between wall and roof is somewhat blurred.

Jaffe is an architect who uses metaphor and poetic image as design tools. To him the house had to catch and reflect some of the dynamism of the dune—itself a wave of sand in slow but constant flux. To him, the massing of the house had to express the tension created between elements that are constrained and elements that are free to soar. Jaffe has tried to bring them together in ways that excite, stir our imaginations, and, metaphysically at least, remind us of those parts of our universal natures that are earthbound and those that are not.

To a surprising and welcome extent, he succeeded.

1977

House in the Sandia Mountains

House in the Sandia Mountains
Albuquerque, New Mexico
Antoine Predock, Architect
1977

At an elevation of over sixty-four hundred feet, this eight-acre site in the Sandia Mountains overlooks in a broad sweep the Rio Grande Valley and distant Mount Taylor to the west. For people who love the outdoors, it is a superb site, and Predock strove to maximize this potential by providing outdoor spaces in the plan for dining, recreation, and watching wildlife on the flank of the adjacent mountain.

The main entry at the east, under the sloping solar roof, falls on a long axis that opens across a covered deck toward Mount Taylor. The main spaces of the house lie just off this axis in a fan arrangement that uses a central circular column as a common radius and produces the circular form seen on the exterior. The kitchen/family room acts as a transition space, both functionally and geometrically, between the living room and the garage. Upstairs are bedrooms and a study that share a small but colorful roof garden.

On the critical faces of the house, Predock has screened out

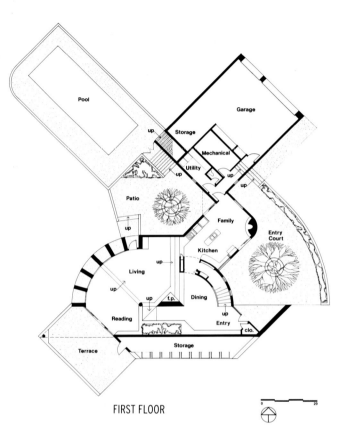

FIRST FLOOR

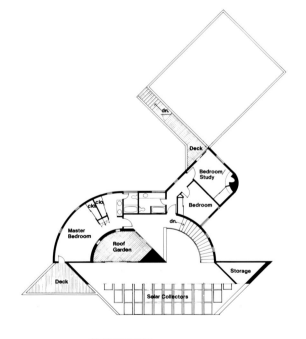

SECOND FLOOR

the bright sun with deep overhangs or narrow slit windows.
The 950 square feet of solar collectors, inclined at forty-five degrees,
are part of a flat plate system that
uses ethylene glycol as a medium.
The solution is circulated from
the collectors to a heat exchanger,
then to a six-thousand-gallon hot
water storage tank. Water in storage is pumped to fan coil units for
space heating. Parallel systems

are used to meet domestic hot-
water demands—and to heat a
swimming pool.

On a site so free of tree cover, in
a region so sunny year-round, the
solar application seems sensible
and efficient. The architect
reports that about eighty percent
of the heat demand (both space
and water) should be met by
the solar system and that the
"recapture time" for initial costs

should be less than fifteen years.
Increased fuel costs could shorten
this period significantly.

In its massing, the house
responds to the traditional architectural forms of the region, and
the admittedly difficult geometry
of arc segments and triangles is
sufficiently resolved to create
highly interesting spaces and
forms that fit this high desert site.

1977

Hulse House

Here is a jewel, a guesthouse and pool built behind the owner's existing house on a suburban street in Atlanta. Though small, the plan provides a rather full range of functions: living room, bedroom, kitchen, dining, two baths, study, and storage. But for the fact that it has only one bedroom, the house is comparable in program to a typical vacation house. A two-story scheme was selected to conserve as much of the site as possible for other activities.

The most desirable view is to the north, overlooking the pool, and therefore this elevation is almost entirely open. The other elevations, by contrast, are essentially windowless to ensure privacy and to reduce solar buildup during warm summer days.

There is considerable tree cover over the house and the neo-Corbusian features of the design—

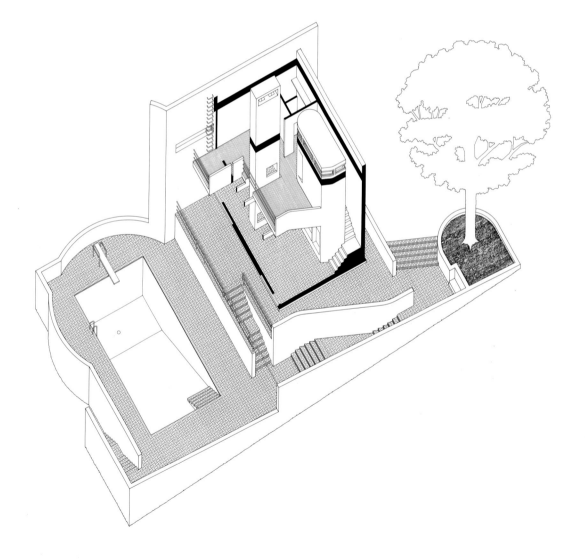

the white wall surfaces in particular—catch the heavy shadows in endlessly shifting patterns. Solar collectors were considered for heating the pool, but it was this same tree cover that made the panels impractical.

The structure of the house is brick veneer over a standard wood frame, except that two-by-six studs were used to accommodate additional insulation in all exterior walls.

The interiors are delicately scaled and detailed with consummate care. Bold primary colors offer powerful contrasts to the white-painted gypsum board partitions and ceilings. So do the brick pavers over the first-floor slab and around the pool.

Inside and out, the Hulse House is invested with fine proportions, rich detail, and the unmistakable stamp of thoughtful design.

1978

Barn on the Choptank

to be celebrated, but they also wanted the barn highly receptive to the sun.

To accomplish these priorities, the architects began by building new exterior walls, fastening them by means of ledger strips to the old plates. New rough siding was also applied and left to weather. Because the old rafters could not support another layer of roofing, the architects nailed two-by-sixes through the existing metal roof into the rafters creating a "T" section that would support new horizontal members and a new metal roof. The cavity this created was filled with insulation.

Along its south wall, the old barn had been built with an integral shed. But the shed cut off long views to the Choptank River as well as winter sunlight, so the architects stripped it of its siding, removed sections of its roof, and in this manner created a trellised

structure that adds enormously to the character of the renovation.

Five solar collectors on the south-facing section of the roof provide domestic hot water, while a conventional oil burner is used for space heating. When the house is unoccupied, the two systems are set in tandem and the thermostat set way down.

"We worked hard," says Mark Simon, "to retain and even enhance the rough-hewn character and yawning openness that make this building a barn, while at the same time giving attention to special places where the inhabitants live and play."

A marvelous renovation.

1978

The owners of this old barn placed some unusual constraints on the architects they commissioned to convert it to a second home. Certain of the constraints, in addition, seemed in a sense to conflict. The owners wanted the renovation to be energy-efficient, for instance, but they also wanted the original siding and roofing to be retained and remain visible from within. They wanted the first-floor structure of stone walls (c. 1850) and hand-hewn timbers

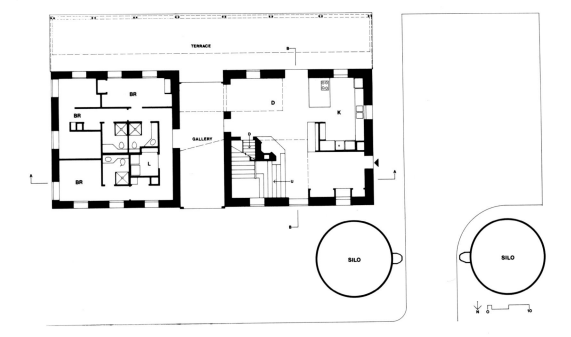

Pallone House

Long low lines with deeply sloping roofs, cantilevered overhangs, and an expansive open plan, all combined with a sensitive respect for landscape and reverence for the nature of materials, powerfully recall Frank Lloyd Wright's Prairie Style; and, indeed, architect E. Fay Jones, who designed this house in central Arkansas, did study for a time at Taliesin.

Closer observation, however, tempers the initial impression and suggests rather that a proper application of Wrightian princi-

ples allows an architect to remain very much his own man and to design buildings of individuality. (Mr. Jones, queried about the Wrightian aspects of his design, demurred politely while granting certain "intangible" influences. "As a matter of fact," he said, "those service cores remind me a little of Louis Kahn's servant space.")

The house, built for a couple with two young sons, is partially sunk into the shore of a private manmade lake and extended over

Pallone House
Central Arkansas
E. Fay Jones, Architect
1978

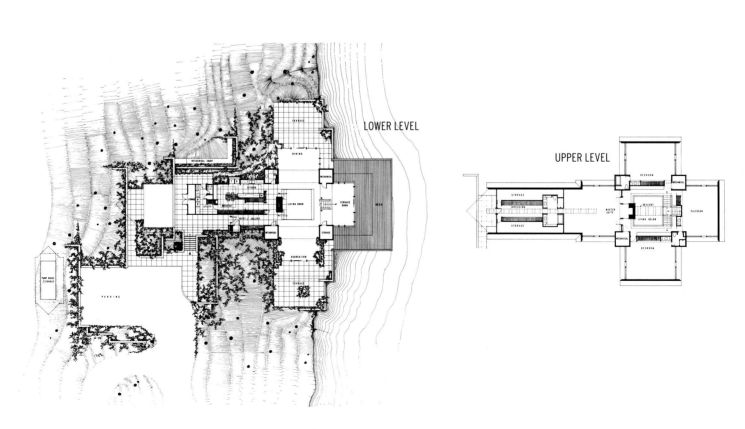

the water on concrete pilings. Its cruciform plan places a two-story living room at the crossing, from which radiate living spaces downstairs and children's rooms upstairs. The strongest defining elements of the plan are four large structural service cores, sheathed with plywood and battens, which support the trusslike cantilevers of the radiating bedrooms and a second-floor gallery that encircles the living room.

Though the steep sheltering roofs suggest from the exterior a perhaps darkened house, the interior is in fact extraordinarily open to light and views of the water and landscape. Entertainment areas on the first floor beneath the cantilevers are glazed on three sides, affording the living room a 180-degree view interrupted only

by the square columns. Upstairs, triangular glass end walls open each bedroom on two sides. Extensive skylights above the central wall and master suite admit additional daylight, as do clerestories connecting the four towers. To reinforce this openness, glass is mitered at the corners of the downstairs rooms and at the ridge of the skylights.

The entry and the second-floor gallery provide exhibition space for the owners' collection of Indian art and relics.

1978

Haupt House

The Haupt House rests squarely on a sandy site surrounded by dune grasses and low greenery. Like other new houses in adjacent oceanfront communities, the Haupt House had to be raised ten feet over mean high water or four-and-a-half feet over existing grade. This produced the opportunity for a series of half levels that the architects exploited with skill. The half levels are linked by a series of stepped ramps that zone apart owners' and guest bedrooms both vertically and horizontally. At the same time, the ramp space produces a tall, very powerful longitudinal volume off which all the other spaces take shape. This plan organization keeps all the circulation space along one wall, allowing primary

Haupt House
Amagansett, New York
Gwathmey Siegel, Architects
1979

living spaces to face south toward the view. By recessing the glazing line on this elevation, the very substantial glass areas are protected from the noontime sun in summer, but admit winter sun deep into the interior spaces.

The geometry of the design bears the firm's signature in its every part, but at the same time there is a good deal that is new, that reflects an evolutionary change in the firm's line of design development. Such signals include the more playful detailing of the fireplace wall, the see-through into the living room, and the elaboration of the handrails along the ramps. Another and even more obvious development is the selection of interior colors. The bright primaries of a few years ago are softened into a range of dark pastels and grays that are used to visually reinforce the intersection of planes and to heighten the sense of layering and density.

The Haupt House is a fine piece of design: its spaces beautifully interrelated, its palette of colors and textures strongly stated, its detailing exquisite throughout.

1979

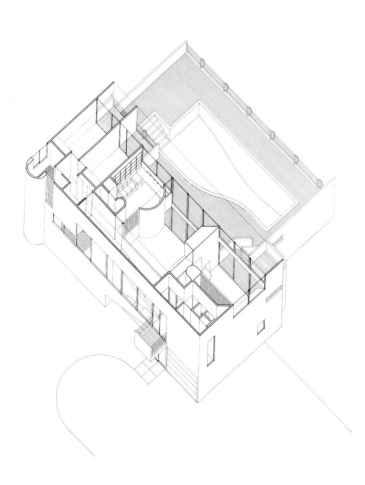

The 1980s and '90s

The 1980s and '90s:

Chipping Away at the Old-Boy Network

CHARLES GANDEE

PRECEDING PAGES:
HOLLYWOOD DUPLEX
LOS ANGELES, CALIFORNIA
KONING EIZENBERG ARCHITECTURE
1988

IZENOUR HOUSE
STONY CREEK, CONNECTICUT
VENTURI, RAUCH AND SCOTT BROWN, ARCHITECTS
1984

Thinking back to the late '70s and early '80s, when I was a wide-eyed young editor at *Architectural Record,* one image comes to mind. And that is the image of the very dapper gentleman-architect Hugh Newell Jacobsen sauntering confidently into *Record*'s offices on the forty-first floor of the McGraw-Hill Building – in early February, if memory serves – with his annual contribution to *Record Houses* tucked discreetly into a black-leather Gucci briefcase.

I remember the receptionist announcing Mr. Jacobsen's arrival and Walter Wagner, *Record*'s editor-in-chief during those years, racing out of his office and greeting his suave, silver-haired old friend, just up from D.C. for the day, like some sort of long-lost fraternity brother – i.e., with a huge smile, a hearty handshake, and a series of hail-fellow-well-met slaps on the back. And then I remember the two men heading off to the light box in the art department and, close on their heels, a cluster of *Record* editors, myself included, who had been hurriedly summoned from their brown-metal Steelcase desks with the excited words, "Come see, Hugh's brought us a house."

As we huddled around, Jacobsen – a man who knows how to work a crowd – ceremoniously unclasped his flashy briefcase and pulled out ten or twelve shimmering color transparencies of his latest house, which he laid on the light box, one by one, and which he was assured would find a home in *Record Houses* that year. Just the way his houses had always found a home in *Record Houses.* And then, after gentleman-architect Jacobsen had treated us all to a tantalizing tidbit or two about the trials and tribulations of designing a new vacation house for Mrs. Onassis on Martha's Vineyard, he and editor-in-chief Wagner headed out for a long wet lunch.

The old-boy network that contributed so much to *Record Houses* for so long began to lose its footing in the early '80s. Which was good news to some, bad news to others. Although the long wet lunches continued, of course, their impact on the magazine lessened. The reason for the change was not so much lapsed loyalty but editorial survival. At a certain point, it had become clear that *Record*'s residential issue – once a much-admired feather in the magazine's cap – had lost much of its luster. This was not a bit surprising considering that what had been conceived and was still being touted as the annual roundup of the year's best houses had devolved – courtesy of a killing combination of nepotism and inertia – into an all-too-predictable roster of architects: another year, another Hugh Newell Jacobsen house.

As early as the late '70s, it was obvious to anyone who was paying attention that the most interesting houses by the most innovative architects were not to be found in *Record Houses,* but in the competition, *Progressive Architecture*. Sad but true, it was *P/A* where young architects looked to find the ideas and themes that would carry them and, indeed, the profession, through the next decade. In other words, in the late '70s, you turned to *Record* to see the work of gentleman-architect Hugh Newell Jacobsen; to *P/A* to see the work of Robert Venturi and Robert A. M. Stern and Frank Gehry and Peter Eisenman and Michael Graves and Rem Koolhaas and Steven Holl and Rodolfo Machado and Jorge Silvetti and Laurinda Spear and Bernardo Fort-Brescia.

If there was a fight between the old guard and the new for editorial control of *Record Houses,* it wasn't, I recall, a particularly fierce one. There was a bit of grumbling in both camps, naturally, but a compromise, it was tacitly agreed, could be worked out whereby a certain number of houses would be selected by one group of editors, a certain number by another group of editors. It was tit for tat, as they say, or at least that's the way I remember it. And it was probably not a bad way to go, considering the usual kind of politics in the profession.

It took a while for the scheme to kick in, for *Record*'s Young Turks to go out and snare the houses they – we – believed best captured the spirt of the time. Certainly, it wasn't yet in effect for *Record Houses* 1980, the dubious highlights of which were an earth-sheltered house in Florida, by William Morgan, who had been designing, as loyal *Record* readers well knew, earth-sheltered

houses in Florida for an impressively long time, and a crisp white gabled house in Pennsylvania by, yes, gentleman-architect Hugh Newell Jacobsen.

Twelve months later, however, it was an altogether different mid-May issue that landed on drawing boards across the country.

Although the cover of *Record Houses* 1981 proudly featured yet another crisp white gabled house in Pennsylvania by gentleman-architect Hugh Newell Jacobsen – we won some, we lost some – there was, among the fifteen other houses inside, ample evidence to suggest that the winds of change had finally reached the forty-first floor of the McGraw-Hill Building. Oh, Brave New *Record Houses,* we thought, congratulating ourselves on snaring Venturi, Rauch and Scott Brown's idiosyncratic variation on the theme of classic Bermuda architecture, Hammond Beeby and Babka's rigorous reworking of Mies van der Rohe's modern tenets, Eisenman/Robertson's up-to-the-1981-minute rendition of the classic Shingle Style, and Bohlin Powell Larkin & Cywinski's homegrown ode to vernacular architecture (opposite).

If 1981 marked the beginning of a newly energized *Record Houses,* it also marked the end of an eleven-year-old tradition, which, in retrospect, would have been better continued. For the first time, the mid-May issue did not contain a portfolio of *Record* apartments, the magazine's annual nod to multifamily housing projects – which had come to be regarded as the architectural equivalent of the homely stepsister. But social and economic concerns were of little concern to many of us then. We, like the profession in general, were preoccupied with style.

We were also preoccupied with personality, with the emerging phenomenon of architect as celebrity. Call it the dawning of the age of *Vanity Fair*.

The early '80s was a time when Michael Graves spent a great deal of time sitting behind desks in Sunar furniture showrooms of his own design, signing autographs for long lines of adoring architecture students who treated him like some kind of postmodern demigod. It was a time when Frank Gehry assumed the mantle of misunderstood cult hero. It was a time when Aldo

GAFFNEY HOUSE
ROMANSVILLE, PENNSYLVANIA
BOHLIN POWELL LARKIN & CYWINSKI, ARCHITECTS
1981

MARTIN HOUSE
KENNETT SQUARE, PENNSYLVANIA
TANNER LEDDY MAYTUM STACY, ARCHITECTS
1993

Rossi in Italy, Mario Botta in Switzerland, and Rem Koolhaas in Holland were heralded as visionaries, as the three wise men from across the sea who would usher us into the promised land. No coincidence that this was the moment when the venerable publishing house of Rizzoli began issuing its apparently never-to-end series of vanity monographs on contemporary architects – an idea conceived by two young draftsmen from Michael Graves's office who would later go on to open a successful advertising agency in Manhattan.

The impact all this had on *Record Houses* was that a name architect – and we all knew which names those were – stood an exponentially better chance of inclusion than a no-name architect. A mediocre Robert A. M. Stern house, for example, was still a Robert A. M. Stern house. And in those days, that was enough.

Guilty of hero worship though we may have been, however, as the '80s ticked along, *Record Houses* also came to represent a platform on which young architects whose names and ideas were not yet known were invited to take a turn in the spotlight. In *Record Houses* 1982, for example, houses by Roger Ferri, Peter Wilson, Harry Teague, and Susana Torre were featured alongside houses by Venturi Rauch and Scott Brown, Gwathmey Siegel & Associates, and, still ticking, gentleman-architect Hugh Newell Jacobsen.

It was an interesting time for design – a period when a lot of things seemed new: History was being rediscovered; context was suddenly significant; regionalism was regarded as a virtue. And although *Record Houses* was beginning to live up to the moment, the magazine itself was still looking a bit dated – an impression, it would be nice to think, that was heightened by its newly invigorated content. In an attempt to bring the old girl up to speed, McGraw-Hill commissioned Massimo Vignelli to redesign the magazine, which he did in time for *Record Houses* 1983. Suddenly, the issue was transformed into a slick glossy that could take its place on newsstands across the country alongside *Architectural Digest*, *House Beautiful*, and *House & Garden* – the mass-circulation shelter magazines that *Record Houses* suddenly found itself competing against – for the prize of publishing, say, Richard Meier's latest million-dollar homage to Le Corbusier.

And so it continued through the '80s, each spring a new crop of *Record* houses. Returning to those issues now, I am reminded of how important it all seemed to us then. Why, I wonder, were we so passionate about getting a tiny little cabin on a hillside in Maine by Bentley/LaRosa/Salasky on the cover in 1983 (page 172)? And why, in 1984, were we so cocky about getting the "exclusive" on Batey & Mack's travertine-clad postmodern villa overlooking the Gulf of Mexico in Corpus Christi (page 186)? Perhaps it was that these houses represented to us the state of the art. They were, we were convinced, the best the profession had to offer. And that, we understood, was the idea behind *Record Houses*.

In retrospect, I wonder if this was enough. In retrospect, I wonder if it would have been worth while for us to have expanded our idea – to have gone beyond the limited formal concerns of architecture, to have paid a bit more attention to the lives these houses were ostensibly meant to accommodate.

I don't recall ever having such doubts during my eight-year tenure at *Record*. It was only later, after I decamped in 1987, that I began to wonder. Where are the people who live in these houses? Why are all these rooms so empty?

And who was the mean-spirited misanthrope who attached the terrible stigma to the word "home"? Whoever he was, he seemed to exert a certain degree of influ-

ence on a number of architects in the late '80s and early '90s who thumbed their noses at conventional/traditional notions of domestic accommodation. Comfort and neighborliness weren't issues that particularly concerned these designers. Their architecture tended to have a hard-edged sensibility to it. Copper- and aluminum-clad surfaces, razor-sharp angles, and battleshiplike facades slid off their drawing boards and into the leafy communities where their clients lived. Damn the neighbors, full speed ahead.

There were notable exceptions to the something-less-than-neighborly trend toward houses as abstract fortifications. But more *au courant* were the houses that stridently eschewed the past in favor of some notion of a heroic future: Josh Schweitzer's quirky assemblage in the California desert (The Monument, page 220), Franklin Israel's bunkerlike Drager House in Oakland (pages 164–5), Koning Eizenberg's introverted duplex in Hollywood (pages 156–7), and Scogin Elam and Bray's sharp-enough-to-cut Chmar House in Atlanta (page 222). These houses are clearly the work of men and women for whom modern sculpture might have been a wise alternative career choice.

Or else they could just be committed to the quaint — and ancient — idea that it is each generation's responsibility to distinguish itself from the generation before.

WRIGHT GUEST HOUSE
SEATTLE, WASHINGTON
JAMES CUTLER, ARCHITECT
1989

Coxe-Hayden House and Studio
Block Island, Rhode Island
Venturi, Rauch and Scott Brown,
Architects
1982

Coxe-Hayden House and Studio

We know these little buildings, sitting alone out in a field. We've seen them before: in an old photograph, in a child's drawing, in other fields. They are a familiar and welcome sight.

Look again. These are not those little buildings.

Initially, they appear as indigenous to the landscape as the stone wall trailing down toward the pond—twin sentinels looking out over the water. For most of us, a "shingle-sheathed box [or two] with gables" will suffice to identify the vernacular; Rhode Island historians, however, will include the "temple" proportions of the facades, and the overscaled bargeboards, to more accurately pinpoint the "countrified Greek

Revival" style endemic to southern New England. But the small house and smaller guest house participate rather than assimilate. They are sophisticated architectural immigrants wearing the local building traditions and materials with the self-confidence and poise of a native.

The windows reveal the other story—the one based on the eleven-page program client Weld Coxe submitted to architects Venturi, Rauch and Scott Brown. Since the house was designed from the outside-in, partner Robert Venturi moved, if not heaven and earth, at least walls and floors to accommodate Coxe's enumerated needs and preferences. The windows register the activity, and the three—not two—floors within. They also provide, by their irregular placement, a magnetic visual charge for the exterior: and by their grand scale, according to Venturi, the little house is made "gracious," not "mean and fussy."

The tension between the general form and the unexpected modifications to that form engages our eye, brings us out of the merely picturesque, invites us in. That play between the familiar and the special is particularly appropriate, considering Coxe's request to "keep it simple, and make it architecture."

Charles K. Gandee, 1982

Hog Hill House

Perhaps we never outgrow the childhood fantasy that some buildings have the faces and personalities of people or animals. Surely we know that if Hog Hill House could talk it would speak with the laconic wit of Maine. The young college professor who lives here with his wife and child grew up nearby, and the designers of their house, though not them-selves Down-Easters, have mastered the local vernacular with artful economy. The project was modest from the start, owing to a tight budget (well under $50,000) and the clients' taste for rural ways.

The couple's affection for Shingle Style cottages, and the contractor's insistence on plain stud-frame construction, led Bentley/LaRosa/Salasky to the basic concept of a rectangular volume with a peaked roof. To minimize clearing on the twenty-six-acre wooded site, designers and owners agreed to build the house at the property's edge, facing a quiet road to the east, and looking out on Hog Hill through forests to the west. Old New England barns suggested the device of a ground floor partially embedded into a gentle slope, with an uphill entrance facing the road and downhill access on grade.

As the plan evolved, a stairwell and chimney (for the wood stove that heats the entire dwelling) became organizing elements within the interior, defining a vestigial "center hall." Living areas and a loft study/music room occupy the upper levels and, to take full advantage of the maximum fourteen hundred square feet the budget allowed, bedrooms were tucked in below, where south windows admit sunlight and meadow views.

Convinced that the exterior needed some distinguishing feature to raise it beyond the banal neatness of a human-size wren house, Ronald Bentley made models to experiment with variations on the peaked roof, even trying on a saltbox for size. In the end,

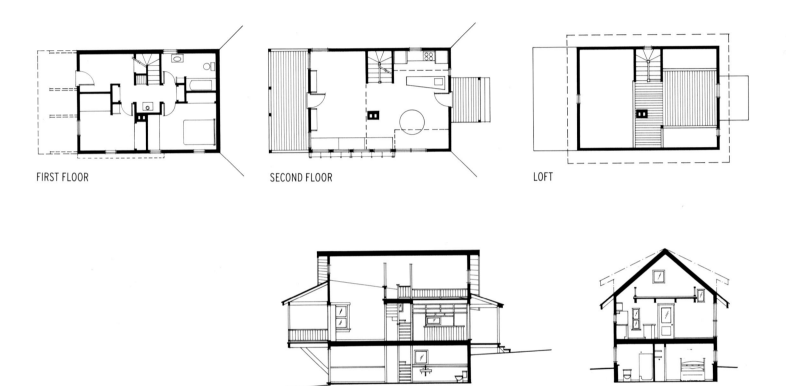

FIRST FLOOR   SECOND FLOOR   LOFT

he settled on a symmetrically warped pitch, created by increasing the height of the side walls from front to back and connecting the rafters from the level ridge beam to the sloping plate atop the walls.

The effect is uncannily suggestive of lifting wings, particularly when seen from the north. "Suddenly, the house seemed to have a definite motion," says Bentley, "as though it were ready to jump off the ground and over the trees to Hog Hill." The taut banded skin of shingles and vertical boards, the beaklike profile of the rear balcony, and corner windows like open eyes reinforce this abstract image of poised animate energy. Here, the house seems to say, is a place where you can rest snug at home, and still hear the call of the wild.

Douglas Brenner, 1983

Hibiscus House
Coconut Grove, Florida
Andres Duany and Elizabeth Plater-
Zyberk, Architects
1983

Hibiscus House

GROUND FLOOR

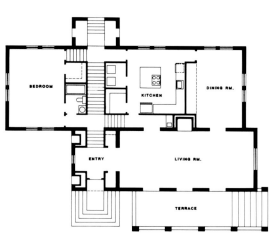

FIRST FLOOR

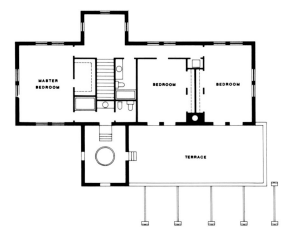

SECOND FLOOR

Discipline, subtlety, restraint, and modesty are qualities all too rare among ambitious young architects, who all too frequently accept their first commission as an invitation to pull out more design stops than is prudent, with results more cacophonous than harmonious. Such is not the case with thirty-three-year-old Andres Duany and thirty-two-year-old Elizabeth Plater-Zyberk, cofounders of the three-year-old Miami firm that bears their names: "We are committed to an architecture which, if not spectacular, promises to be of lasting value." And while the Hibiscus House does fall into that dubious first-commission category, and while Duany and Plater-Zyberk are comfortably "young" and duly ambitious, the speculative residence they began their portfolio with is, true to the promise, "not spectacular." Conversely, it is neat and serene and elegant. Though neat and serene and elegant do not generally constitute high architectural praise, they do if the

architecture is an unwelcome late entry into a venerable (by Miami standards) neighborhood that already has all the housing stock it would like, thank you, and would have preferred the private tennis court on Hibiscus Street to remain a private tennis court. South Florida real estate, however . . .

Minus the "real" client and/or program that would have helped shape the Hibiscus House, Duany and Plater-Zyberk looked to the immediate neighborhood for design inspiration. The local 1930s Spanish vernacular, with its faint tinge of Bauhaus, clearly caught their eye—and their design, quite intentionally, looks as if Addison Mizner had met Adolf Loos on Hibiscus Street. The stripped-down, flat-roofed, modified-hacienda style is not only appropriate to Coconut Grove, but to the "rich South American family" targeted for the house; the smooth stucco-over-concrete block is no less appropriate to the developer's fifty-two-dollars-per-square-foot budget.

Duany and Plater-Zyberk attacked the problem of how to squeeze a 4,020-square-foot house onto a small and awkward triangular site by breaking down the mass—dividing the house into three graduated volumes that "gesture to the site." However, this slipped geometry contains an axial, somewhat formal plan, with the entry raised a half level above grade (allowing a maid's room to be tucked underneath),

and floor-level changes between first-floor living areas and bedroom offering clear separation of public and private spaces. The symmetry and enfilades of the plan reinforce the air of formality —more in keeping with Latin American tradition than the open plans typical of recent south Florida construction.

Charles K. Gandee, 1983

Spiller Houses

Spiller Houses
Venice, California
Frank O. Gehry & Associates,
Architects
1983

Jane Spiller first met Frank Gehry when she was researching a film about Los Angeles artists and he was building a house and studio for the painter Ron Davis. Impressed by Gehry's enthusiasm and the sculptural vigor of his work, Spiller sought him out several years later when she decided to build a house of her own in Venice. The project was a test of skill (and enthusiasm) for architect and owner alike. Gehry adroitly satisfied his client's program for two dwellings (one for rental tenants) on a thirty-by-ninety-foot urban lot and gave her privacy, sunshine, and views of the Pacific shore a block away. Spiller successfully interpreted Gehry's schematic design to city and state zoning authorities and later helped supervise construction.

Gehry's earliest model roughed out two rectangular boxes of different heights—the lower rental house to the south, and Spiller's towerlike residence to the north—linked across one side of a courtyard. Besides forming a visual transition between existing bungalows to the east and a four-story apartment building to

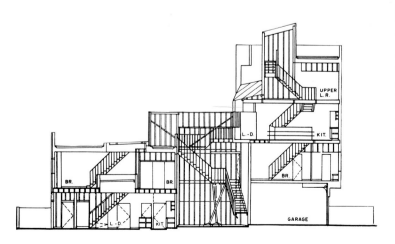

the west, this staggered setback combined maximum density and favorable exposures. As the design evolved, it became ever more sculptural in the interlocking of corrugated-metal-clad volumes and the penetration of light through structure. In plan, the completed pair of houses is virtually devoid of right angles, echoing the slanted parallelogram of the site and Gehry's abiding preoccupation with oblique Constructivist form.

The interior is essentially an open loft, with circulation and specific functional compartments deployed at the edges of a vertical core. Skylights and windows animate this space with shifting patterns cast by the sun—an almost cinematic effect that marks a logical step beyond Gehry's previous experiments with direct and reflected light in his own Santa Monica house. The exposed-stud structure that constituted only one element in that busy collage has expanded here into an all-inclusive aesthetic.

Gehry has long admired the balloon-frame construction characteristic of the Los Angeles area and believes it has an inherent beauty that too often disappears when it is covered up. In revealing the skeleton of the Venice house he produced a tectonic analog to the ever changing light show within, a quality he describes as "the spontaneity of wood . . . I wanted the whole house to look as if it was in process." Such spontaneity is, of course, hardly ingenuous. When Jane Spiller and the contractor began selecting lumber, Gehry recalls, "I was worried they'd make it more finished than I intended."

Douglas Brenner, 1983

FOURTH (ROOF) LEVEL

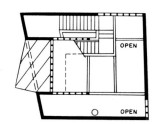

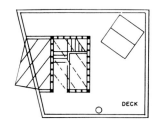

THIRD LEVEL

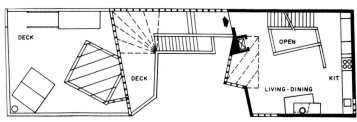

SECOND LEVEL

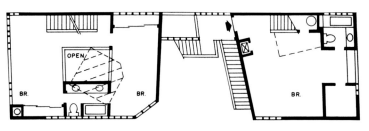

FIRST LEVEL

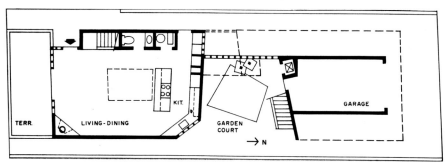

House on Lake Memphremagog

Though no longer the sole preserve of rail barons and their peers, the northern reaches of Lake Memphremagog retain much of their seigneurial wilderness. Some of the choicest territory bordering the thirty-mile-long lake, which extends from Quebec into Vermont, has been held for generations by the family that commissioned Peter Rose to replace an Edwardian country house destroyed by fire. The owners reside in Toronto, and their children are grown, but since the lakeside property is still a year-round family gathering place, everyone hoped that the new house would embody some palpable link with the old.

Rose willingly consented to reuse the earlier building's majestic site, a rock-walled terrace high above a secluded point. But rather than archaeologically reconstruct the vanished lodge, whose interiors had in fact been gloomy and inconvenient, he extracted a few salient features—restrained classical ornament, prominent gables, and French doors giving onto porches and balconies—to evoke fond memories in an otherwise original scheme.

Rose's originality is not the sort that thrives on egotistical bravura, a stance that would have offended both the spirit of the place and his clients' temperament. His design is at once patrician and homey, sweetly echoing the English strains of Webb, Voysey, and early Lutyens, reinterpreting them with exquisite sensitivity to nuance. Verandas and board-and-batten walls give a North American complexion to a scheme that also honors old-world decorum. The tall gables, crisply detailed siding, and decorative embellishments of the porticoed "main house," which is oriented toward the prime views, contrast with the low hip roofs and plain, battered stucco walls of the rear service area. Rose has

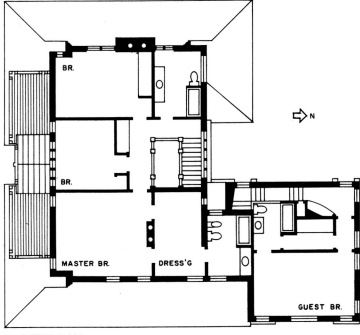

SECOND FLOOR

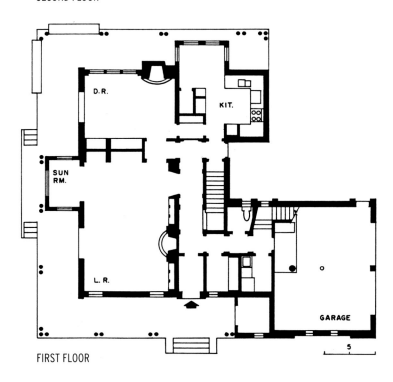

FIRST FLOOR

nonetheless joined "master" and "servant" with interlocking bays, continuous roof planes, and bands of casements, stringcourses, and cornices. Symmetry and asymmetry are counterpoised in a shifting equilibrium that also distinguishes the axial plan.

Picturesquely irregular in its overall configuration, the layout is experienced in the round as a cadenced progress through harmonious suites of rooms. Each chamber is at once a still point of serenity in itself and the juncture of ordered vistas beyond its walls. This is eminently a house with *rooms*, not "spaces," and the two-story stair hall at its heart is more than a passageway; it is a stately arena for the entrances and exits, the greetings and farewells, that ritually bind a family to its home.

Douglas Brenner, 1984

Villa on the Bay
Corpus Christi, Texas
Batey & Mack, Architects
1984

Villa on the Bay

It is surprising that a climate as extreme as Corpus Christi's has failed to produce a generally accepted local style of architecture. Yet a tour of the city's bayside residences reveals only the usual all-American suburban hodgepodge—from misplaced Cape Cod to sprawling '50s modern.

California architects Andrew Batey and Mark Mack didn't help matters either when they tackled their commission for this house on the Texas coast. Instead of attempting to invent the missing regional vernacular—responsive to Corpus Christi's

torrid summers, bitter winters, and fierce annual hurricane season—Batey and Mack simply looked to the site they were given, a not-so-gentle knoll rising from the bay, and then turned (as is their practice) to a suitable archetype—in this case, the Roman villa. More specifically, Batey and Mack chose the villa suburbana as their model, since the classic duality between introverted public facade and extroverted garden front seemed made to order for their site, wedged as it is between four-lane Ocean Drive and an unobstructed view of Corpus Christi Bay.

Once the contrasting aspects of the two facades had established a historical prototype, the antique villa theme was reinforced through classical proportions keyed to a unifying geometric order: an insistent four-foot grid reflected on the floor plane (in inlaid slabs of marble), on the wall (in aediculae), and on the ceiling plane (in coffers). And true to their sources, Batey and Mack defined a powerful central axis that dominates the entire plan. First established in the open-air atrium just inside the street entrance, the eight-foot-wide axis passes through a varied sequence of open and closed spaces, and rather than terminate this stately promenade

with the obvious climax of a grand lookout window on the bay, the architects extended an imperial avenue right down to the water's edge.

Although they take pride in the respectful references to classical precedent that include such details as Roman grilles, porticoes, and pergolas, Batey and Mack are most pleased with the solid masonry construction that gives the house its venerable monumentality—and helps to temper the inhospitable climate. No Nubian slaves were required to hoist the three-eighths-inch Italian travertine tiles onto the concrete block frame, but the effect comes as close to the glory that was Rome as any Texas Maecenas could wish.

Charles K. Gandee, 1984

House on the Northeastern Coast

Private House
Northeastern Coast
Graham Gund Associates, Architects
1984

fantasy that has been stripped of all traditional ornament. The dormers, placed in seemingly random fashion on all four elevations, function admirably by exploiting both intimate and expansive vistas into the surrounding landscape. One such projection appears to have slipped off the roof and become embedded in the ground just outside the dining room where it frames a perfect nineteenth-century seascape and defines the edge of a small patio.

Given the exuberance of the exterior, the rather straightforward nature of the interior is something of a surprise, and one is quickly reminded that the structure's curving walls enclose what is essentially a simple cube. The three-story vertical arrangement of the space in fact has a citified quality not unlike an urban townhouse—that is, until one takes a whiff of the salt air and peers out one of those dormers toward the distant New England hills.

Paul M. Sachner, 1984

The setting is a barrier island located a few miles off the coast of New England. Long shorelines, virgin forests, deep harbors, and windswept dunes come into sharp focus as the ferry from the mainland approaches. No teeming resort this place—only a simple boat landing, a tiny village centered on a triangular green, and a collection of summer cottages that for generations have sheltered residents of Boston, New York, Hartford, and Providence seeking an escape from their weekday labors.

If the idyllic character of its location so close to the hectic northeastern megalopolis is an anomaly, the seasonal retreat that Graham Gund Associates has designed for a young couple from Boston is likewise idiosyncratic. Although the clients had a fairly typical program for the 2,125-square-foot house—living and

dining rooms for entertaining, a master bedroom and two guest chambers for visitors, and screened porches for eating and sleeping during warm weather—they also sought architectural imagery at once distinct from and in harmony with the other summer residences on the island.

There are, to be sure, some obvious historical allusions to nineteenth-century seaside architecture at work in a house that consists of a huge cedar-shingled mansard roof dotted with an array of white clapboard dormers, bays, and porches. It is just as apparent, however, that the dwelling is no archaeologically precise imitation of past forms. Seen from the water's edge, the roofhouse (as it has been dubbed by both the architect and owner) rises mysteriously out of a low bluff like the Brobdingnagian belvedere of some Victorian

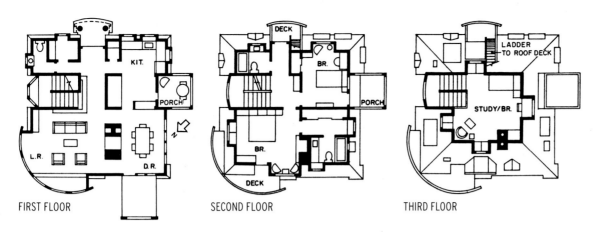

FIRST FLOOR   SECOND FLOOR   THIRD FLOOR

Norton House
Venice, California
Frank O. Gehry and Associates,
Architects
1985

Norton House

Venice, California. Envision a place where food stamps are as common as platinum American Express cards will soon be, and where the carriers of each have managed to effect an uneasy truce at best. Envision a place where a generation of wanderers came to hang out in the, '60s, burned out in the '70s, and stayed on to cool out in the '80s. Envision a place where those who can't make it in the L.A. fast lane downshift into idle, and where record moguls who find Santa Monica too suburban and Malibu too far away carefully try to hide their irritation when asking the welfare mother who lives next door to *please* keep her kids off the red BMW. Envision a place where the professionally unemployed wile away the cloudless blue days following superannuated flower children handing out save-the-world pamphlets, while mad-at-the-world punks with Mohawk haircuts sneer at Arnold Schwarzenegger's old buddies pumping iron on their bench presses by the sea. Envision a place where balding blond beach boys pretend the summer hasn't ended and go right on looking for that perfect wave. Now envision all that implies.

It's a ten-minute stroll from Frank Gehry's office to Bill Norton's house. This being greater Los Angeles, of course, you could drive, but it's better to go on foot—at least the first time. You'll take Ocean Walk, the city's hurly-burly pedestrian thoroughfare, and along the way you'll get a crash course in the sorrows and joys of what sociologists would

term "a transitional community with a heterogeneous population." If the decibel level at which Venice blares its socioeconomic cacophony explains why some horrified visitors seek lurking in its tortuous streets a ready indictment against the errors of our fast-track society's ways, it also explains why architect Frank Gehry remains so loyal to the place. Venice is for Gehry an intensified microcosm of the American city—warts and all—and the American city is where this architect practices architecture. Though he hasn't built much here, Gehry never forgets Venice in his work: it is his source of inspiration, storehouse of raw material, and context of choice. To the squeamish, he might point

out that we do not live in a perfect world, so why pretend.

For Bill Norton, who spent his youth keeping close watch over the bronzed California girls immortalized in song, Venice is understandably sentimental. And though Norton climbed down from his lifeguard tower and headed for Hollywood years ago, he returned to a one-story stucco cottage on the beach after an early brush with success. When bachelorhood ended, and the second generation was imminent, Norton turned to longtime friend Gehry for help at home.

"Does it stand out?" asks Gehry, who will be heartbroken if you answer in the affirmative. For it was his intention to remodel and expand Norton's ramshackle

THIRD FLOOR

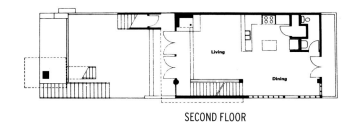

SECOND FLOOR

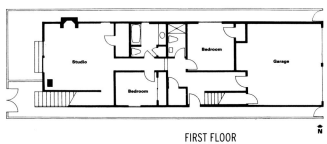

FIRST FLOOR

cottage without interrupting the abrasive fabric of its environs. Like an acquisitive beachcomber, Gehry gathered up the bits and pieces that compose Venice, and then, with the hand of a sculptor, reassembled them. Most recognizable in his palette of found objects is the lifeguard tower perched above the sky-blue tile ground-floor studio. The diminutive study is not only a winsome reminder of screenwriter Norton's well-spent youth, but a practical lookout from which he can search sand and sea for the elusive muse.

As backdrop for the tower, which has become a much-loved local landmark, Gehry replaced the former cottage's courtyard and garage with a three-story box that houses the bulk of Norton's three-thousand-square-foot program. Though Gehry is better known for assemblage than appliqué, a $180,000 budget forced him to forgo the former in favor of the latter. Even so, the vivid juxtaposition of polychromatic tile and stucco, with corrugated metal and chain-link appurtenances, suggests that Gehry is uncompromised by the change. A final bow to the neighborhood is revealed on the south facade, where Gehry expressed his need "to make relationships . . . to form connections" by specifying glass, not stucco or tile. "I don't do Disneyland," asserts a remorseless Gehry: "I do what I do, and my career suffers or gains by it. But that's me, and that's what I do."

Charles K. Gandee, 1985

Prince House

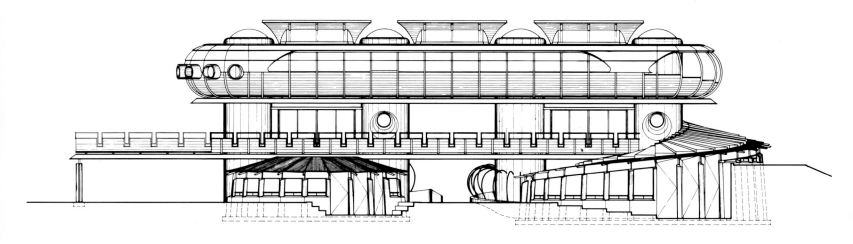

Those seeking inspiration for a contextual vacation house on Cape Cod or a glass-and-steel Miesian pavilion in one of the better suburbs should turn back now, and quickly. For we are about to embark on "a journey of the mind," as Rod Serling might put it, a voyage into the imagination that will take us far from the cozy domesticity of the neo-Shingle Style or the serenity of mainstream modern. We are entering the highly personal world of Bart Prince, whose own house on a quiet residential street in Albuquerque exemplifies the architect's place within the tradition of American architectural expressionism.

Although some observers see his buildings simply as biomorphic or space-age fantasies sprung full-grown from the overactive mind of a child of the '50s, there is much more at work in Prince's

architecture than an artist's comic-book conceptions of the future. Born of the Southwest, Prince has been subjected to a whole range of visual stimuli—both natural and manmade—that may have profoundly affected his work. Albuquerque's quintessentially garish Route 66 strip, the stark lunar landscape of New Mexico, and the powerful imagery of nearby pueblos and kivas might easily lead one to believe that almost anything is possible on the high plateau.

That impression was reinforced at Arizona State University, where Prince first immersed himself in the work of Frank Lloyd Wright and later, Bruce Goff, whose idiosyncratic buildings seemed in harmony with Prince's own notions of design. After graduation Prince spent four years in Goff's office, and although he left his mentor in 1972 to set up his

own practice, their relationship remained close right up to Goff's death in 1982. (That relationship, in fact, continues today with Prince's supervising the completion of Goff's last design, a new museum of Japanese art in Los Angeles.)

In the manner of Goff, Wright, and even Sullivan, Prince's buildings express the individual character of his clients, and for his own four-thousand-square-foot house that character is inextricably intertwined with the architect's debt to his three progenitors. The geometry of circles and spirals that preoccupied Wright from the 1940s onward is evident throughout Prince's house, from two round ground-floor living and studio spaces and four structural cylinders supporting the capsulelike upper story, to circular concrete columns rising from the building perimeter and cylin-

drical solar collectors that warm the bedroom area.

Sullivan's experimentation with metal ornament is brought up to date with the spiky steel rods that Prince utilized as a frame for solar shading fabric and as a "feathery transition between the house and sky." Underlying the building's odd shape (some see it as a rocket ship, others a caterpillar) is the architect's claim that the actual form evolved from the inside out: the curving upper-level walls are a result of Prince's desire for soft, comfortable interiors and are not based on any pre-conceived formalistic ideas.

Despite the unwavering support of his clients, Prince's buildings do have their critics, particularly those who feel that all architecture in New Mexico should be of the brown-stucco-to-look-like-adobe school. (One fanatical detractor went so far as to burn down Prince's Santa Fe studio three years ago.) What the naysaying contextualists fail to

see, however, is that Prince is the latest in a long line of American originals—Goff, Wright, Soleri—whose work seems to flower with special brilliance in the desert sun. Seen in that light, his house is firmly rooted in the history of the freewheeling Southwest.

Paul M. Sachner, 1985

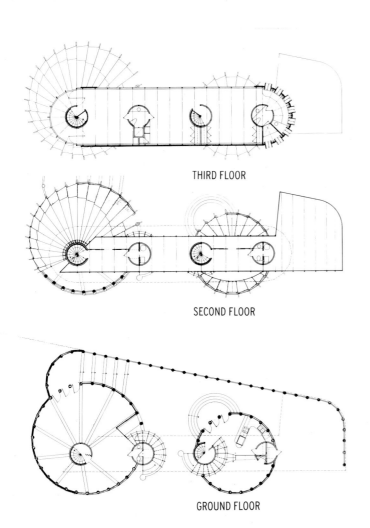

THIRD FLOOR

SECOND FLOOR

GROUND FLOOR

Casa Los Andes

Casa Los Andes
Lima, Peru
Arquitectonica International
Corporation, Architect
1986

With Inca pyramids only a block away, modernist high-rises around the corner, and Mission Revival haciendas cheek by jowl with Bauhaus villas up and down the street, one searches in vain for a "typical" building style in the neighborhood of Arquitectonica's Casa Los Andes. If there is one architectural form that binds together this fashionable quarter of Lima, it is the garden wall that demarcates every property line— nowadays a matter of practical security as much as local tradition. The twelve-foot-high protective barrier surrounding Arquitectonica's site conforms exactly to this cultural matrix, while isolating a neutral field for aesthetic invention.

Viewed from a nearby apartment tower, the cruciform structure skewed within this oblong frame looks uncannily like an axonometric drawing plucked from the architects' Miami office. Stucco walls precisely delineate that taut constructivist equipoise of Arquitectonica's graphics, while transforming them into a three-dimensional object of voluptuous plasticity and vibrant color. Looking down with a giant's eye, one can imagine lifting this exquisite artifact to turn it around in one's hand. Head-on, at human scale, there is no single vantage point from which the structure composes a static hierarchy of masses or facades.

Instead the house resembles some cubist assemblage, a cluster of intersecting planes and curved and polygonal volumes, whose unifying order changes constantly as one passes around and through them. In Lima, where

land is scarce and even mansions are impacted into narrow lots, the dynamism of Arquitectonica's habitable sculpture seems positively exuberant.

The crossed walls that trace the geometric coordinates of the house also imply centrifugal lines of force, figuratively turning the confines of the yard inside out and reorienting them to the points of the compass. Besides opening the interior to light, air, and Pacific breezes, this *parti* effectively fuses architecture and landscape to extend their perceptible reach. Discipline prevails, however, since this schema also divides both house and garden into visually and functionally related quadrants: a flower-edged dooryard adjoining the foyer; a lawn and terraces outside the living room; an orchard bordering the library, dining room, and kitchen; and a service court off the laundry and maids' quarters. The neat domestic economy is reminiscent of old-fashioned handbooks for the gentleman builder, albeit phrased in a modernist idiom. The result recalls the streamlined "modernistic" abodes of the 1930s,

whose machine-age decor encased amenities for a way of life that, in retrospect, seems almost quaintly old-world.

Nevertheless, by current upper-class Peruvian standards, the Casa Los Andes is a remarkably casual and efficient home. The owners, a young couple with two small children, asked for a compact layout with easy circulation, multi-use rooms, and ample spaces for outdoor living. Architects Laurinda Spear and Bernardo Fort-Brescia (who is Peruvian by birth) interpreted these desiderata with proper regard to local mores. While their thirty-five-hundred-square-foot layout dispenses with the customary suite of ceremonial reception rooms segregated from everyday family areas, it still includes a self-contained service zone complete with back stairs. And though the glass-walled living room and indoor/outdoor dining areas relax conventional boundaries, the public aspect of the entire compound is impeccably reserved.

From the street, only a red-trimmed portal hints at the spectacle beyond the garden wall. Inside the front yard, the pink entry pavilion flanked by jutting wings looms like a gatehouse, standing guard before the inner sanctum. A porthole and tiny diamond windows, seemingly punched at random through the curvaceous tower, merely intensify the enigma. Even when the house door is open, the visitor's field of vision is confined to a sky-lighted stairwell. Only on the threshold of the living room does a subtle shift of axis at last reveal exhilarating vistas through the family's private domain. This dramatic route of arrival lends magic to the secret garden beyond, where a venerable date palm presides over the mysteries of modern art like a faithful native retainer.

Douglas Brenner, 1986

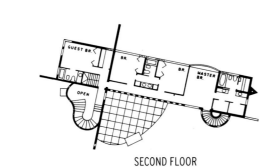

SECOND FLOOR

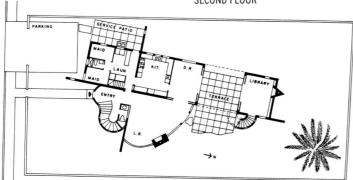

FIRST FLOOR

Farmhouse in Connecticut

Classicism is a serious business for Allan Greenberg. His architecture has little to do with the ironic and witty plays on classical themes that are so common in this age of postmodern flamboyance—in its way, Greenberg's architecture is as far from postmodernism as the work of Mies van der Rohe. Indeed, there is something not unlike Mies in Greenberg's work: it, too, is a kind of Platonic quest for perfection in a certain language, and it, too, emerges out of a deep conviction that there is a right way to make architecture. This sprawling Georgian house on a rural site in Connecticut exemplifies Greenberg's stance. It is an ambitious and grandiose house, larger by half than the Mount Vernon that inspired it, and altogether lacking in the curious mix of sophistication and provincialism that energizes Mount Vernon. This house

is made all of knowledge, not of instinct; it is a measured, sober essay in classicism, its every dormer and bracket emanating an erudite love of classical architecture. But, for all its deliberate quality, this house in not "about" classicism, as the classicizing designs of so many of Greenberg's peers might be said to be; Greenberg is more interested in practicing the classical language than in commenting on it.

It is difficult, for all the importance of the architectural issues this house raises, not to speak first of its scale, for a house of this stature would be impressive in any mode today. The main wing is roughly 120 feet long, with attached side pavilions large enough to permit a full-size swimming pool to be within one of them. It commands its expansive, rolling site with self-assurance, presenting its grander

facade containing a full-length portico to the open landscape and its more restrained front to the entry drive. The building is thus in the tradition of country houses that open primarily to their gardens and that, despite their rural or semirural settings, offer a formal, almost urban, face at their front door.

But most direct, of course, is the connection between this house and Mount Vernon and, by implication at least, to such descendants of Mount Vernon as Stanford White and Theodate Pope Riddle's Hill-Stead. Greenberg did not copy Mount Vernon literally; he not only changed the scale significantly, he altered many of the details. The entry facade is cleaned up considerably, and made symmetrical. The most conspicuous result of both the increase in size and the greater order is to create a sense of vast, clean space; the white-painted facade with its false rustication seems to go on and on. But it feels as if it were pulled taut over this large form—there is a precision to Greenberg's detailing that keeps this mass from appearing bloated.

It is not hard to sense Greenberg's love of the Italian Baroque here; he has more than just acknowledged the relationship between Italian classicism and American Colonial architecture, he has intentionally exaggerated it. And it is through all of this that the facade acquires the rhythms that bring it to life: such details as the molding around the oval window in the central pediment, the huge brackets that anchor each end of the pediment, and the composition of Ionic pilasters and sumptuous scroll-

work over the front door together bring a rich texture, and create a kind of drama in a facade that, without them, could run the danger of being precise to the point of primness. The entry facade thus has a kind of positive tension; it is almost a dialectic between a precise and highly ordered version of American Colonial architecture and the more sensuous, brooding power of the Baroque.

On the garden facade, however, there is no such tension—a colonnade of paired Tuscan columns sets a gentle rhythm, and the detailing is understated. The mood is quieter here; despite the grandeur of the columns, this facade is clearly a less formal front, a great veranda open to the landscape rather than a portico. Greenberg's decision to pair the columns was critical; it gives this

facade a rhythmic proportion that it would otherwise lack, as well as looking back to classical precedent before American Colonial architecture, as the Baroque allusions in the entry facade do.

The formality of the entry facade is enhanced by the presence of the two side wings, which are placed at right angles to that facade to form what is in effect a three-sided forecourt. Graceful curving arcades do much to energize this outdoor space, which is defined and partially enclosed on its fourth side by careful planting of trees. The side wings are detailed in a manner consistent with the main house; they acknowledge their subsidiary status not only by their placement and scale, however, but by a slight understatement of detail. One side wing contains a garage and

service function; the other, essentially similar on the exterior, contains the swimming pool. It is not a little startling to find a swimming pool behind Palladian windows, though the barrel-vaulted space that it has been given makes a successful transition from the architectural themes of the structure itself to the mood of an indoor pool, for it gives the space a clear but unaggressive monumentality.

The plan is rigorously formal. A central hall spans the house from front to back, and on the rare occasions when the doors are left open, the view through the house from one landscape to another is an extraordinary one of nature placed securely within Greenberg's classical frame. The rooms are large, but not overwhelming; if anything, they seem the result of an attempt to strike a careful balance between normal domestic scale and the rather larger scale of this house. Despite Greenberg's oft-professed affection for the work of Lutyens, he has kept all eccentricity of interior space far away from here. There are no double-height or round spaces or tricks of any kind. It is in tiny phrasings of detail rather than in grand gestures of space that Greenberg's ability to manipulate the classical language is most convincing. (It is here, too, that the remarkable quality of workmanship in this house is most apparent.) The chimneypieces alone tell the story: In the sitting room used as an informal family gathering place, a mantlepiece emerges with utter restraint and control from walls paneled in the same wood. In one of the two more formal living rooms, the voltage is turned up a bit in a somewhat more elaborate mantel with dentil moldings, while in the library, the main living room, the mantel is supported on brackets and the chimneypiece decorated with a band of circles. In another room, meanwhile, the mantel is Adamesque.

The cornice moldings are one of Greenberg's favorite variations on classical precedent. Unlike most cornices, in which brackets along each side stop short of the corner, which remains a void, some of Greenberg's cornices have an extra bracket on the diagonal, to visually bring the molding around the corner. So, too, above the arched window on the main landing has he topped pilasters and architrave with diagonal modillions. It is not exactly an earth-shattering event—but it is a significant reminder that Greenberg remains committed to using classicism as a vocabulary within which he can invent, not as a source that he must only take literally. What also prevents this house from becoming cloyingly "Colonial" was the decision of the owners, who are noted collectors of postwar American art, to display their collection here amid American antiques. Thus there are such startling presences as an Andy Warhol portrait of Marilyn Monroe above one of the fireplaces, a Lichtenstein in the entry hall, and Warhol's Mona Lisa sharing a wall on the main stair with a grandfather clock.

These juxtapositions work in part because of the high quality of the collection—just any modern

art would hardly be at home in a setting of this caliber—and in part because the leap over time they represent helps this house to transcend the limits of any period design. So, too, with the important Art Deco furniture that the owners brought from their previous residence (a Robert Venturi house completed in the early 1970s), which fills a sitting room in this house, entering into easy, if unusual, dialogue with the architecture that enriches both. The modern art and the Art Deco furniture in effect make more conspicuous and easier to understand the point made by Greenberg's inventiveness of detail—that this is not a piece of colonial Williamsburg, but a structure built in the 1980s. It was not only made in our time, it was conceived for our time: Allan Greenberg's belief is not that classicism is something of the past that our age would do well to return to, but that it is as much a living and changing style as any other.

Paul Goldberger, 1986

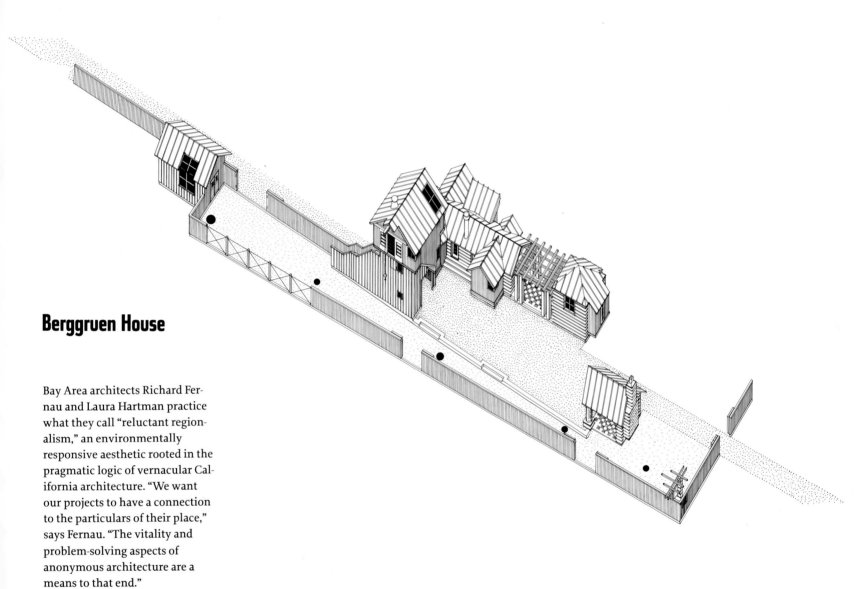

Berggruen House

Bay Area architects Richard Fernau and Laura Hartman practice what they call "reluctant regionalism," an environmentally responsive aesthetic rooted in the pragmatic logic of vernacular California architecture. "We want our projects to have a connection to the particulars of their place," says Fernau. "The vitality and problem-solving aspects of anonymous architecture are a means to that end."

A vivid example of the partners' philosophy is the house they designed for painter Helen Berggruen in the Napa Valley. Fernau and Hartman began the project by studying the ramshackle farmworkers' housing that once stood on their site, a wooded lot sandwiched between two creeks on the edge of a vineyard. This casual setting inspired them to design a rustic camp of separately housed functions, including a bunkhouse, cookhouse, and lodge, that was eventually consolidated into an L-shaped building

focused on a central outdoor space. Segmented into corrugated-metal-clad bays and a tower, the house evokes the accretionary spirit of the original sheds in a linear organization of discrete rooms that allows the client and her guests to live and work independently from one another.

Fernau and Hartman anchored the compound to its natural boundaries by clearly defining an axial relationship between their various components. From the driveway, bordered by a workshop and fenced yard, the house is entered through a doorway at the base of a tower, which also provides access to a courtyard with an outdoor fireplace. To the southeast, the architects ordered the main spaces of the house as an enfilade of study, living room, and kitchen that is connected by a pergola to a freestanding bedroom/bathroom pavilion. From this central spine, they projected gabled, glazed bays of varying proportions that distinguish each room with an individual character and provide views to the surrounding vineyards. To connect the main block of the house to the master bedroom and painting studio, Fernau and Hartman followed the example of their admired vernacular sources. They simply roofed over the stairway leading from the entrance hall and affixed a metal staircase to the side of the tower's upper story—a bold, unpretentious maneuver that exemplifies the structure's rigorous simplicity.

Deborah K. Dietsch, 1989

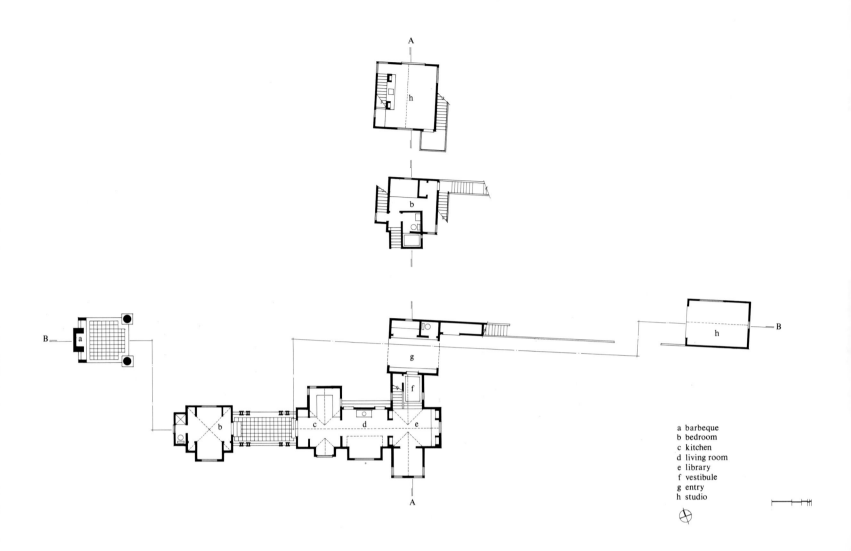

a barbeque
b bedroom
c kitchen
d living room
e library
f vestibule
g entry
h studio

The Monument

The Monument
Joshua Tree, California
Schweitzer BIM, Architect
1990

Los Angeles architects love the desert, but few have actually tried to build there. Now young architect Josh Schweitzer has constructed his first ground-up building in the high desert of Joshua Tree National Monument. What's more, he has used this commission as a chance to state the case for an architecture that he has only been able to make in fragments in Los Angeles itself. Beyond its isolated site, this small "monument," as Schweitzer calls it, proposes some new basic forms for the architecture of southern California.

There are really two landscapes at Joshua Tree, the vast desert preserve three hours east of Los Angeles. One is the stark wilderness of stacked boulders and surreal detail of every cactus, thorn bush, and prickly flower that inhabits this otherworldly grandeur. Then there is the town of Joshua Tree and the other fast-growing desert communities—fragmented Western settlements buried beneath an absurdly scaled paraphernalia of shopping centers, corner malls, and ranch homes.

It would be hard to miss the small compound Schweitzer has erected between the town of Joshua Tree and the park entrance, in a valley of huge boulders dwarfing small homes. It is made up of an orange outdoor pavilion, an olive-green living area, and a royal-blue bedroom wing. The blocks are placed like three man-made boulders piled up in contradiction to both the natural stones and the manmade shelters. Each piece is cut with openings at odd angles, making the scale and composition of the compound even more abstract. It is an alien, willful piece of architecture.

The Monument comes from, stands outside of, and comments on both the natural and the the manmade landscapes. That is exactly how Schweitzer planned this weekend retreat for himself and four friends, who together own three successful restaurants and an eyewear business in Los Angeles. "What struck me about Joshua Tree was that the rocks were majestic, and that I was building in between the rocks. So I tried to make it look as if these blocks had been left after everything else had slid down." What is found in between those rocks is

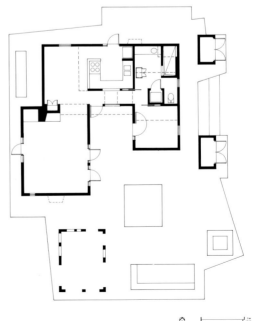

a wood-frame fragment of the formal complexities of civilization, here liberated from too much program. There is only one tiny bedroom, along with two sleeping lofts. The orange pavilion is an outdoor room, a place of shade and idiosyncratic pattern, the living room merely about verticality in a landscape of horizontal expanse. The forms are large, blocky, and deformed, existing somewhere between orthogonal rationality and the rough-and-tumble world outside. Each carefully placed window frames a view of the mountains, but in a cut-off, angled manner, so that the desert is seen through edited snapshots.

When asked about the colors, Schweitzer points out: "Everyone thinks of the desert as monochromatic, and so people try to blend in. But when you look carefully, there are all these amazing colors: a vivid green lichen growing on a rock, a bright red flower, and the impossibly blue sky. This compound takes those colors and builds them at the scale of man, which is bigger than the flowers, but a lot smaller than the rocks."

The compound "confronts the city with the desert," adds Schweitzer, but in fact it confronts the memory of the city with the memory of original desert, monumentalizing them into an architectural fusion. The forms may seem primitive, but they are derived from sources like Schweitzer's former employer, Frank Gehry, and the work of Luis

Barragan. Its urbanity is stripped down to the bare essentials: stucco and gypboard walls, redwood windows, offbeat colors, and furnishings that wed Scandinavian modern and Midwestern rural. The house is a prime example of "the New Primitivism," a knowing adaptation of the Los Angeles vernacular and a retreat into quasi-naive, quasi-muscular shapes eschewing both decoration and the semblance of coherence.

It is perhaps fitting that the first monument to this movement should be constructed at the place where the fragmented vernacular is still nascent and the most extreme version of the California landscape is preserved. The Joshua Tree compound is an inventive, romantic revision of both California landscapes and a statement of a new world that might be found within and beyond the opposition of those worlds. Schweitzer talks about the compound not as just shelter, not "a tent in the desert, but a church, a cathedral, a place of mystery." It is a ceremonial, if perhaps somewhat pretentious, beginning for a young architect—the kind of small, beautiful piece of architecture that the amorphous world of southern California building deserves.

Aaron Betsky, 1990

Chmar House

Chmar House
Atlanta, Georgia
Scogin Elam and Bray, Architects
1991

Designing buildings that defer to nature without becoming completely subservient to it is one of architecture's greatest challenges. Mack Scogin, Merrill Elam, and Lloyd Bray achieved this in the four-thousand-square-foot house they recently completed for Tod and Linda Chmar. Their feat owes as much to the skill of the three architects as the merits of the Chmars' property—2 ¾ wooded acres next to a nature preserve, just three miles from downtown Atlanta. And in what may seem like a bit of divine intervention, space for the house was made nature's way, by a fallen tree.

The fortuitous clearing was not lost on the architects, whose assignment for their first residential commission was to provide an open living room, dining room, and kitchen, the usual assortment of bedrooms, and accommodations for visiting parents, and, at the same time, to disturb the site as little as possible. The architects responded by raising the volume of the main house

into the foliage on concrete foundation walls that step down to the north, leaving the hillside otherwise untouched.

Nearly perpendicular to the main house is a semidetached guest wing that spans the driveway, creating a sheltered entrance and carport. In plan, the house resembles an open switchblade, its sharp edge a master-bedroom balcony poking into the woods. In elevation, the house is a visual sleight of hand: from a distance, the wood-framed structure, coated in a hybrid cementitious stucco finish the color of army camouflage, disappears, leaving redwood window frames as the only remaining traces of its presence among surrounding oaks.

In organizing the interiors of the main house, which is 130-feet long and bulges to twenty-feet

wide in the living room, Scogin looked to the spirit, if not the exact form, of the architecture of Japan, where the Chmars themselves find daily inspiration. Indeed, the clients' practice of Japanese rituals touches not only the removal of shoes after entering the front door (where the architect actually built a low bench and shoe rack), but also includes the daily "giving and receiving of light" in a Goshinden room, which houses an ancestral altar.

Scogin arranged the rooms according to ceremonial use and meaning: the long staircase to the Goshinden room, immediately visible upon entry, cannot be reached until one passes down the hallway and up steps into the "heart" of the house, where it hovers above the living-room

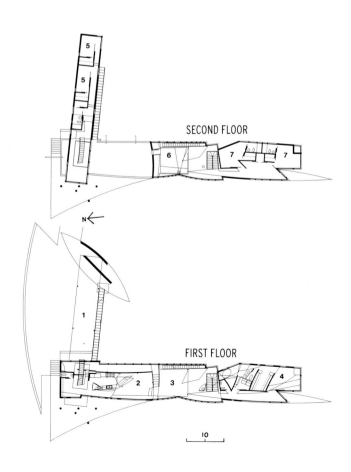

SECOND FLOOR

FIRST FLOOR

seating area as a birch and glass shell. Opposite the Goshinden room staircase is the hallway to the master bedroom, lit by a ribcage of windows swelling out into the woods, creating a forced perspective toward the sharp prow of the master-bedroom balcony. Another staircase leading to second-floor bedrooms, current domain of baby Ian, is hung from

the ceiling joists by steel rods and is framed by birch and plywood panels that resemble pressed flower petals.

The architects adeptly blurred the transition between inside and outside by specifying a variety of window sizes and shapes, which frame views of massive tree shafts as well as adjacent parts of the house. Daylighting is generous

throughout the house and often used to dramatic effect. For example, skylights bathe the back walls of the Goshinden room, and holes in a nearby glass-encased wood door transmit an otherworldly glow from outside. The ground plane of the house sweeps out into the woods in a triangular deck off the kitchen, punctuated by five sixty-foot-high leaning telephone poles, which, like the house itself, are both firmly planted and freely soaring.

Karen D. Stein, 1991

LIST of ALL RECORD HOUSES by ARCHITECT

Abbot, Carl
1972: Sarasota, FL
Abbot, Richard Owen
1969: Westbrook, CT
Aeck Associates
1958: Callaway Gardens, GA
Allen/Buie Partnership
1982: Longview, TX
Allen, Gerald
1982: New Jersey
Ames, Anthony
1978: Atlanta, GA
Amsler Hagenah MacLean
1985: Nottingham, NH
Anderson, Barbara & Allan
1972: Rye, NY
Andrus, Moulton
1978: Park County, WY
Anderson/Schwartz
1990: Rutherford, CA
Anshen & Allen
1956: San Rafael, CA
1960: Sunnyvale, CA
Arango, Jorge
1970: Miami, FL
Architects Collaborative
1957: Bedford, MA
1959: Provincetown, MA
1961: Northern Massachusetts
Architects Design Group
1971: Harrison, NY
Architectural Resources Cambridge
1972: Lincoln, MA
Arley Rinehart Associates
1976: Perry Park, CO
Arquitectonica International
1986: Lima, Peru
1989: Glencoe, IL
1989: Cook County, IL
Astle, Neil & Associates
1972: Wausau, NE
1977: Nebraska
Aydelott, A. L. & Associates
1959: Helena, AK
A 2 Z
1987: Seattle, WA
Bahr Hanna Vermeer & Haecker
1975: Fremont, NE
Baker & Blake
1971: Annandale-on-Hudson, NY
Baker Rothschild Horn Blyth
1979: Philadelphia, PA
Baringer, Richard E.
1958: Highland Park, IL

Barnes, Edward Larrabee
1957: Mount Kisco, NY
1959: Chappaqua, NY
1967: Connecticut
1968: New York State
1976: Mt. Desert Island, ME
Barnes, Edward Larrabee & Armand P. Avakian
1984: Texas
Barnstone, Howard & Eugene Aubry
1965: Houston, TX
Barnstone, Howard
1973: Galveston, TX
Barron, Errol
1980: New Orleans, LA
Batey & Mack
1984: Corpus Christi, TX
Bassetti & Morse
1962: Mercer Island, WA
Beadle, Alfred N.
1965: Phoenix, AZ
Becker, Robert
1980: Mercer Island, WA
Beckett, William S.
1956: Beverly Hills, CA
Behn & Gavin
1973: Santa Cruz County, CA
Behn, Peter
1979: Berkeley, CA
Bentley/LaRosa/Salasky Design
1987: Virginia Beach, VA
1988: Bucks County, PA
1993: East Holden, ME
1993: Westchester County, NY
Bennett & Tune
1970: Lexington, KY
Berke, Deborah & Carey McWhorter
1993: Hillsdale, NY
Berkes, William J.
1964: Wayland, MA
Betts, Hobart
1970: Londonderry, VT
1974: West Hampton, NY
1975: Englewood, NJ
1976: Vermont
1977: Long Island, NY
1979: Quogue, NY
Biltmoderne
1988: Williamstown, MA
Binkley Associates
1964: Glencoe, IL
Birkerts, Gunnar & Frank Straub
1961: Northville, MI
Birkerts, Gunnar & Associates
1968: Grand Rapids, MI
Bissell & Wells
1979: Nantucket Island, MA

Blackwell, Marlon
1991: North Carolina
Bliss & Campbell
1963: Minnesota
1964: Minneapolis, MN
Bloodgood, John D.
1969: Des Moines, IA
Blum, Vanporciyan & Mitch
1972: Franklin, MI
Bohlin and Powell
1976: West Cornwall, CT
Bohlin Powell Larkin & Cywinski
1981: Romansville, PA
Bolton & Barnstone
1956: Houston, TX
1957: Houston, TX
1959: Houston, TX
Bolton, P. M. & Associates
1963: Houston, TX
Botta, Mario
1986: Morbio Superio, Switzerland
Booth/Hansen & Associates
1983: Northville, MI
1984: Chicago, IL
1990: Lake Bluff, IL
Booth, Laurence
1980: Evanston, IL
Booth & Nagle
1970: Chicago, IL
1972: Minnesota
1974: Des Moines, IA
1975: Vashon Island, WA
1976: Hinsdale, IL
Booth, Nagle & Hartray
1978: Glencore, IL
Breuer, Marcel & Associates
1956: Andover, MA
1958: Duluth, MN
1960: Andover, MA
1961: Baltimore, MD
1978: South Orange, NJ
1979: Big Sur, CA
Breuer, Marcel & Herbert Beckhard
1967: Litchfield, CT
1981: New Canaan, CT
Brillembourg & Lanman
1984: Sagaponack, NY
Brooks & Carey Architects
1992: Monkton, VT
1995: Westby, WI
Brooks, Turner
1988: Nazareth, PA
1988: Litchfield County, CT
Browne, Robert B.
1958: Key Biscayne, FL
1961: Miami, FL
1962: Key Vaca, FL
Browne, Robert B. & Rufus Nims
1960: Miami Beach, FL

Brownson, Jacques C.
1956: Geneva, IL
Bruck, F. Frederick
1965: Cambridge, MA
Bruder, William
1977: Arizona
1993: Phoenix, AZ
Buff, Straub & Hensman
1961: Los Angeles, CA
Bull Field Volkmann Stockwell
1972: San Francisco, CA
1978: Napa Valley, CA
Bull, Henrik
1964: El Dorado Hill, CA
BumpZoid
1983: Flint Hill, VA
Bunshaft, Gordon
1966: East Hampton, NY
Burger & Coplans
1973: San Francisco, CA
Burk, Lebreton & Lamantia
1958: Lake Charles, LA
Burley, Robert Associates
1973: Maine
Burr, Andrus F. & A. K. McCallum
1988: Williamstown, MA
Bystrom, Arne
1980: Whidbey Island, WA
Caldwell, James E., Jr.
1975: Woodside, CA
Callender, John Hancock
1957: Darien, CT
Callister, Payne & Bischoff
1976: Belvedere, CA
Campbell & Wong & Associates
1964: Colusa, CA
Cannady, William T.
1973: Houston, TX
1981: Round Top, TX
Cardwell, Richard
1977: Puget Sound, WA
Carver, Norman F., Jr.
1960: Kalamazoo, MI
1961: Kalamazoo, MI
1962: Kalamazoo, MI
Ceraldi, Theodore M. & Associates
1989: Rockland County, NY
Chafee, Judith
1970: Connecticut
1975: Tucson, AZ
1979: Arizona
Chapell, Don
1977: East Hampton, NY
Chatham, Walter
1989: Seaside, FL
Cheng, James
1977: Vancouver, BC

Chimacoff/Peterson
    1973: Montauk, NY
    1976: Morristown, NJ
Chrysalis Corp.
    1983: Chicago, IL
Citterio/Dwan Studio
    1990: Japan
Clark & Menefee
    1988: South Carolina
    1990: Charleston, SC
Colbert, Charles
    1965: New Orleans, LA
Combs, Earl B.
    1971: Fire Island, NY
Conklin, William J.
    1959: Peeksville, NY
Copland, Hagman, Yaw
    1980: Aspen, CO
Corbett, Mario
    1957: Healdsburg, CA
Coston, Truett H.
    1954: Oklahoma City, OK
Crissman & Solomon
    1977: New York State
    1979: New Vernon, NJ
    1981: Massachusetts Coast
    1983: Center Lovell, ME
    1984: Northwestern Connecticut
Crites & McConnell
    1973: Burlington, IA
Cuetara, Edward
    1974: Martha's Vineyard, MA
Curtis & Davis
    1956: Pascagoula, MS
    1957: New Orleans, LA
    1959: New Orleans, LA
    1960: New Orleans, LA
    1964: New Orleans, LA
Cutler, James
    1989: Seattle, WA
    1989: Port Blakely, WA
    1992: Lew Beach, NY
Daland, Andrew
    1970: Lake George, NY
Damora, Robert
    1962: Cape Cod, MA
Darrow, Lee Stuart
    1960: Mill Valley, CA
Dart, Edward D.
    1963: Highland Park, IL
    1966: Lake Forest, IL
Davis, Brody & Associates
    1972: Westport, CT
Davis, Brody & Wisniewski
    1957: Huntington Valley, PA
    1959: Peeksville, NY
Davis, Mary Lund
    1964: Tacoma, WA
Dean/Wolf Architects
    1995: North Castle, NY
Design Consortium
    1978: St. Paul, MN

Designers & Builders
    1957: Greenwich, CT
Desmond, John
    1960: Hammond, LA
DeVido, Alfred
    1969: East Hampton, NY
    1972; Westchester County, NY
    1975: Long Island, NY
    1976: Long Island, NY
    1978: Watermill, NY
Dorman, Richard L.
    1959: Encino, CA
    1967: Sherman Oaks, CA
Dickinson, Duo
    1985: Madison, CT
Duany, Andres & Elizabeth Plater-Zyberk
    1983: Coconut Grove, FL
    1984: Key Biscayne, FL
    1986: Key Biscayne, FL
Edwards & Portman
    1965: Atlanta, CA
Eck, Jeremiah
    1982: Newton, MA
Eisenman/Robertson
    1981: Eastern Long Island, NY
Elliot, Cecil D.
    1956: Mt. Airy, NC
Ellwood, Craig
    1959: Mailbu, CA
    1964: West Los Angeles, CA
Elting, Winston
    1965: Ligonier, PA
Englebrecht, Robert Martin
    1966: San Rafael, CA
Erickson, Arthur
    1975: Vancouver, BC
Erickson/Massey
    1969: Cotuit, MA
Ernest, Robert
    1962: Atlantic Beach, FL
    1995: Santa Monica, CA
Faulkner, Avery C.
    1966: McLean, VA
Ferri, Roger C.
    1982: Water Island, NY
    1987: Greenwich, CT
Fernau & Hartman
    1984: Sonoma County, CA
    1989: Rutherford, CA
Field, John L.
    1961: Los Altos Hills, CA
Fisher-Friedman Associates
    1965: Millbrae, CA
    1966: Belvedere, CA
    1972: Belvedere, CA
    1981: Santa Clara, CA
Fisher, Frederick
    1987: Los Angeles, CA
Fisher, Nes, Campbell & Partners
    1966: Baltimore, MD
    1969: Owing Mills, MD
Fitzpatrick, Robert E.
    1976: St. Helena, CA

Fitzpatrick, Kirby Ward
    1969: Yorktown, NY
Flansburgh, Earl R.
    1965: Weston, MA
    1966: Dover, MA
    1967: Harvard, MA
    1968: Weston, MA
    1973: Lincoln, MA
    1975: Cape Cod, MA
Fletcher, William
    1958: Portland, OR
Forbes, Peter
    1983: Mt. Desert Island, ME
    1986: Mt. Desert Island, ME
    1987: Mattaposett, MA
    1989: Great Cranberry Island, ME
Foote, Steven
    1980: Connecticut
Franzen, Ulrich
    1956: Rye, NY
    1958: Rye, NY
    1959: Rye, NY
    1960: Essex, CT
    1962: New London, CT
    1963: Greenwich, CT
    1964: Westport, CT
    1966: New Canaan, CT
    1967: Long Island Sound, NY
    1968: Long Island, NY
    1979: Bridgehampton, NY
Gehry, Frank O.
    1983: Venice, CA
    1985: Venice, CA
Gelardin Bruner Cott
    1977: Massachusetts
George, F. Malcolm
    1968: Berkeley, CA
Gibbs, Hugh & Donald Gibbs
    1970: Palos Verdes Peninsula, CA
Gilchrist, John Robert
    1963: Lakewood, NJ
Gill, Crattan
    1980: Cape Cod, MA
Glass, Frank B.
    1964: Des Moines, IA
Gluck, Peter L.
    1973: Westminster, VT
Goetz & Hansen
    1959: Lafayette, CA
Goldfinger, Myron
    1971: Waccabuc, NY
    1974: New York State
    1978: Chappaquiddick Island, MA
Gonzales, Bennie M.
    1967: Paradise Valley, AZ
Goodman, Charles M.
    1956: Lake Barcroft, VA
Gordon B. Varey
    1963: Seattle, WA
Goubert, Delnoce Whitney
    1967: Morris Township, NJ

Gregory, Jules
    1961: Lambertville, NJ
    1963: Verona, NJ
    1966: New Jersey
Greenberg, Allen
    1986: Connecticut
Grider & La Marche
    1959: Boise, ID
Griffith, Newton E.
    1962: Edina, MN
Grossman, Theodore A., Jr.
    1971: Parker, CO
Growald, Martin
    1971: New York State
Gruber, Morton M.
    1969: Atlanta, GA
Gueron, Henri Charles
    1972: East Hampton, NY
Gund, Graham
    1979: Massachusetts
    1983: Boston, MA
    1984: Northeastern Coast
Gustavson, Dean L.
    1960: Salt Lake City, UT
Gwathmey & Henderson
    1968: Purchase, NY
    1969: Manchester, CT
Gwathmey, Henderson, Siegel
    1970: Orleans, MA
Gwathmey Siegel & Associates
    1973: East Hampton, NY
    1975: Eastern Long Island, NY
    1979: Amagansett, NY
    1981: Cincinnati, OH
    1982: Long Island, NY
    1995: Zumikon, Switzerland
Haid, David
    1968: Lakeside, MI
    1971: Evanston, IL
Haigh Space
    1985: Remsenburg, NY
Hallberg, Joan
    1994: Stewart's Point, CA
Hammond Beeby and Babka
    1981: Portar County, IN
    1987: Wilmette, IL
Hampton, Mark
    1960: Savannah, GA
    1964: Tampa, FL
    1968: Tampa, FL
Hariri & Hariri
    1993: New Canaan, CT
    1995: Ontario, Canada
Harris, Steven
    1991: Kent, CT
    1992: Ormond Beach, FL
Heimsath, Clovis B.
    1966: Nassau Bay, TX
Hellmuth, Obata & Kassabaum
    1959: St. Louis, MO
    1961: Ladue, MO
Henderson, Richard
    1972: Huntington Bay, NY

Hester-Jones & Associates
   1963: Del Mar, CA
Hirshen & Van Der Ryn
   1969: Point Reyes, CA
Hisaka, Don
   1976: Ohio
Hiss, Philip
   1958: Sarasota, FL
Hobbs Fukui Associates
   1978: Seattle, WA
Holmes, D. E.
   1972: Tampa, FL
Howard, Coy & Company
   1988: Chino, CA
Hovey, David
   1985: Venice, CA
Hunter, E. H. & M. K.
   1956: Manchester, NH
   1960: Hanover, NH
Huygens and Tappé
   1972: Barrington, RI
   1974: Darien, CT
   1980: New England Coast
Ilmanen, William J.
   1968: Baltimore, MD
Isozaki, Arata
   1987: Venice, CA
Israel, Franklin D.
   1993: Los Angeles, CA
   1995: Oakland, CA
Ito, Toyo
   1986: Tokyo, Japan
Jacobs, Donald
   1978: Sea Ranch, CA
Jacobsen, Hugh Newell
   1964: Bethesda, MD
   1965: Riva, MD
   1966: Martha's Vineyard, MA
   1967: Washington, DC
   1968: Bristol, RI
   1969: Washington, DC
   1970: Montgomery County, MD
   1971: Easton, MD
   1973: Salisbury, CT
   1975: Philadelphia, PA
   1976: Frederick, MD
   1977: Chevy Chase, MD
   1978: Washington, DC
   1979: Wayzata, MN
   1980: Pennsylvania
   1981: Central Pennsylvania
   1982: Eastern Shore, MD
   1984: Maryland
   1986: Lima, OH
   1989: Long Island, NY
Jacobson, Philip
   1975: Seattle, WA
Jaffe, Norman
   1964: Lake Mahopac, NY
   1971: Sagaponack, NY
   1977: Long Island, NY
   1978: Old Westbury, NY

Jennewein, G. P. & J. J.
   1963: New York, NY
Jimenez, Carlos Architectural Design
   1990: Houston, TX
   1994: Houston, TX
Johansen, John MacL.
   1956: New York, NY
   1958: Connecticut
   1976: Connecticut
Johansen-Bhavnani
   1978: Connecticut
Johnson, Philip
   1957: Irvington-on-Hudson, NY
   1962: Long Island, NY
Johnson, Roy Sigvard
   1961: Hastings-on-Hudson, NY
Jones, A. Quincy & Frederick E.
Emmons
   1956: Pacific Palisades, CA
   1957: San Mateo, CA
Jones, E. Fay
   1978: Arkansas
Jones, E. Fay & Maurice Jennings
Architects
   1990: Evergreen, CO
Jones, Walk C., Jr.
   1953: Memphis, TN
Jones, Walk + Francis Mah
   1969: Memphis, TN
   1971: Memphis, TN
Kaplan, Richard D.
   1970: Montauk Point, NY
Katselas, Tasso
   1964: Pittsburgh, PA
   1974: Pittsburgh, PA
Keck, George Fred & William Keck
   1958: Olympia Fields, IL
   1962: Pleasant Valley, PA
   1963: Highland Park, IL
   1966: Burlington, IA
   1967: Chicago, IL
Kelly, John Terence
   1962: Elyria, OH
Kessler, William & Associates
   1973: L'Arbre Croche, MI
   1976: Lakeport, MI
   1981: Southeastern Michigan
Keyes, Lethbridge & Condon
   1961: Washington, DC
   1966: Bethesda, MD
Killingsworth-Brady-Smith
   1958: Long Beach, CA
   1963: Long Beach, CA
Kindorf, Robert
   1976: Plumas County, CA
Kirk, Paul Hayden
   1957: Seattle, WA
   1961: Bellevue, WA
Kirk, Wallace, McKinley & Associates
   1970: Mercer Island, WA

Kliment, R. M. & Frances Halsband
   1985: Westchester County, NY
Knorr & Elliott
   1958: Atherton, CA
   1963: Tahoe Keys, CA
   1974: Riverside, CA
Koch, Carl & Associates
   1963: Yorktown Heights, NY
Koning Eizenberg Architecture
   1988: Los Angeles, CA
   1995: Santa Monica, CA
Kramer & Kramer
   1956: Maplewood, NJ
   1962: Teaneck, NJ
Kroeger, Keith Associates
   1979: Westchester, NY
Kroeger, Keith & Leonard Perfido
   1971: Waccabuc, NY
Krueger, Paul H.
   1973: Truro, MA
Kuhn & Drake
   1962: South Plainfield, NJ
Lake/Flato Architects
   1991: Chicago, IL
Lamantia, James R.
   1969: New Orleans, LA
Land & Kelsey
   1962: South Laguna, CA
Landsberg, William W.
   1957: Long Island, NY
Larson, Thomas
   1974: Roseau, MN
Lautner, John
   1971: Malibu Beach, CA
   1977: Acapulco, Mexico
Lawrence, Saunders & Calongne
   1957: New Orleans, LA
   1958: New Orleans, LA
Lee, Roger Associates
   1962: Berkeley, CA
Leedy, Gene
   1965: Rockledge, FL
Legorreta, Arquitectos
   1991: Los Angeles, CA
Leela Design
   1979: Guilford, CT
Lewis, George S.
   1962: Westport, CT
Liebhardt, Frederick & Eugene
Weston III
   1965: Del Mar, CA
Lipsey, William
   1984: Aspen, CO
Lindstrom & Morgan
   1993: Boston, MA
Little, Robert A.
   1956: Plymouth, OH
   1957: Cleveland, OH
Lovett, Wendell H.
   1969: Bellevue, WA
   1972: Mercer Island, WA
   1974: Crane Island, WA

Lubowicki/Lanier
   1984: Los Angeles, CA
Luckenbach, Carl
   1965: Birmingham, MI
Lundy, Victor
   1958: Venice, FL
   1959: Sarasota, FL
Mackall, Louis
   1976: Nantucket, MA
Mack, Mark
   1988: Sausalito, CA
   1989: Santa Monica, CA
Machado & Silvetti Associates
   1994: Concord, MA
Malone & Hooper
   1957: Kentfield, CA
Marquis & Stoller
   1970: Marin County, CA
Massdesign
   1979; Westford, MA
Matsumoto, George
   1957: Raleigh, NC
   1961: Roanoke Rapids, NC
   1962: Sedgefield, NC
Mayers & Schiff
   1970: Hawley, PA
   1974: Armonk, NY
   1980: Long Island, NY
McCue Boone Tomsick
   1973: San Mateo County, CA
McKim, Paul W.
   1968: San Diego, CA
McLeod, James
   1972: Fire Island Pines, NY
Meathe, Kessler & Associates
   1961: Franklin Hills, MI
   1965: Grosse Pointe, MI
Meier, Richard
   1964: Essex Falls, NJ
   1968: Darien, CT
   1969: East Hampton, NY
   1977: Westchester, NY
Merrill, Simms & Roehrig
   1961: Honolulu, HI
Merz, Joseph G. & Mary L.
   1969: Brooklyn, NY
Metz, Donald
   1974: Lyme, NH
   1982: Medfield, MA
Millar, C. Blakeway
   1975: Georgian Bay, Ontario
   1980: Toronto, Ontario
Miller/Hull, Partnership
   1991: Decatur Island, WA
Millett, Mark
   1984: Seattle, WA
Mills & Martin
   1971: Dublin, NH
Mills, Willis N., Jr.
   1967: Van Hornesville, NY
Mithun, Ridenour & Cochran
   1960: Issaquah, WA

MLTW/Moore-Turnbull
    1967: Monterey, CA
    1969: Santa Cruz, CA
    1970: Pajaro Dunes, CA
    1973: Sea Ranch, CA
MLTW/Turnbull Associates
    1972: Aptos, CA
    1983: Kauai, Hawaii
Mockbee/Coker/Howorth
    1992: Madison County, MS
Moger, Richard B.
    1967: Clayton, NY
    1973: Southampton, NY
Molny, Robin
    1975: Aspen, CO
Moore, Arthur Cotton
    1972: Washington, DC
    1977: Arlington, VA
    1980: Washington, DC.
Moore, Charles W. & Richard C. Peters
    1962: Corral de Tierra, CA
Moore Grover Harper
    1978: Guilford, CT
    1978: Maryland
    1979: Sagaponack, NY
    1980: Connecticut
Moore Ruble Yudell
    1981: Los Angeles, CA
Morse & Harvey
    1981: Rye, NY
Morgan & Lindstrom
    1979: Bainbridge Island, WA
    1983: Boston, MA
Morgan, William
    1963: Atlantic Beach, FL
    1965: Jacksonville, FL
    1966: Ponte Vedra Beach, FL
    1968: Atlantic Beach, FL
    1974: Jacksonville, FL
    1976: Florida
    1977: Florida
    1980: Florida
Morris, Langdon
    1960: Aspen, CO
Morton, David & Thomas Cordell
    1992: Petaluma, CA
Muchow, W. C.
    1957: Denver, CO
Myers, Barton
    1977: Toronto, Ontario
Nagle, Bruce D.
    1985: Bridgehampton, NY
Nagle, Hartray
    1982: Door County, WI
Nagle, Norman C.
    1957: Minneapolis, MN
Nelson, George & Gordon Chadwick
    1958: Kalamazoo, MI
Nelson, Ibsen A. & Russell B. Sabin
    1963: Seattle, WA
Nemeny, George
    1957: Long Island, NY
    1963: Long Island, NY
    1967: Rye, NY

Neski, Julian & Barbara
    1968: Long Island, NY
    1969: Amagansett, NY
    1971: Bridgehampton, NY
    1972: East Hampton, NY
    1973: Remsenburg, NY
    1975: Ashley Falls, MA
    1982: Eastern Long Island, NY
Neuhaus & Taylor
    1958: Houston, TX
Neutra, Richard J.
    1956: Los Angeles, CA
    1961: Los Angeles, CA
Newman, Herbert S.
    1965: Woodbridge, CT
    1985: Woodbridge, CT
Newman, Richard & Judith
    1975: Fire Island, NY
Nichols, Robert
    1974: Austin, TX
Nims & Browne
    1956: Miami, FL
Nims, Rufus
    1957: Redington, FL
Norten, Enrique
    1992: Mexico City
Noyes, Eliot
    1956: Hobe Sound, FL
    1957: New Canaan, CT
    1959: Port Chester, NY
    1971: Stamford, CT
    1974: Greenwich, CT
Oakland, Claude
    1964: Orange, CA
    1968: Sunnyvale, CA
Obata, Gyo
    1967: St. Louis, MO
O'Herlihy, Lorcan
    1987: Malibu, CA
Olcott, Schliemann & Simitch
    1988: Bucks County, PA
Oliver, James C.
    1973: Portland, OR
Olsen, Donald
    1966: Ross, CA
Oppenheimer, Brady & Lehrecke
    1963: Tappan, NY
Osmon, Fred Linn
    1979: Carefree, AZ
Ossipoff, Vladimir
    1960: Honolulu, HI
    1963: Honolulu, HI
Overpeck, Frazier
    1957: Santa Monica, CA
Owen, Christopher H. L.
    1975: Westchester County, NY
    1979: Long Beach Island, NJ
    1980: Stockbridge, MA
Pasanella, Giovanni
    1969: Winhall, VT
    1970: Wellfleet, MA
Pearson & Porter
    1973: Atlanta, GA

Pei, I. M.
    1964: Washington, DC
Pekruhn, John E.
    1956: Fox Chapel Borough, PA
    1958: Pittsburgh, PA
Perfido, Leonard P.
    1976: Weston, CT
Perry Dean Roger & Partners
    1991: Nevis, West Indies
Perry, Lyman
    1977: Pennsylvania
Phillips, Frederick Associates
    1990: Chicago, IL
    1990: Washington Island, WI
    1995: Chicago, IL
Porter/Kelly
    1978: Atlanta, GA
Predock, Antoine
    1977: New Mexico
    1982: Santa Fe, NM
    1986: Albuquerque, NM
    1990: Paradise Valley, AZ
    1994: Dallas, TX
Prentice & Chan, Ohlhausen
    1970: Riverside, CT
Price, Robert Billsbrough
    1959: Tacoma, WA
Prince, Bart
    1985: Albuquerque, NM
    1989: Albuquerque, NM
    1991: Orange County, CA
Pulliam, Matthews & Associates
    1973: Beverly Hills, CA
Quinn, Richard E.
    1966: Denver, CO
Quigley, Rob Wellington
    1984: San Diego, CA
    1989: Temecula, CA
Rader, Morton
    1975: Marin County, CA
Rapson, Ralph
    1959: St. Paul, MN
    1966: Wayzata, MN
Redroof Design
    1982: Fairfield County, CT
Ream, Quinn & Associates
    1968: Denver, CO
Riley, J. Alexander
    1971: Inverness, CA
Riley, Jefferson B.
    1983: Western Pennsylvania
Rivkin/Weisman
    1983: Fire Island, NY
Roark, Donald R.
    1966: Goldon, CO
Robbin & Railla
    1966: Burbank, CA
Rockrise, George T.
    1958: Medford, OR
    1960: Atherton, CA
Roland-Miller
    1978: Napa, CA
Rolando, Charles R.
    1980: Carlisle, MA

Rosenfeld, Michael
    1984: Lincoln, MA
Rose, Peter
    1984: Austin, Quebec
Ross, Michael
    1981: Old Westbury, NY
Roth, Harold & Edward Saad
    1970: Cheshire, CT
Roth & Moore
    1980: Woodbridge, CT
Rudolph, Paul
    1956: Auburn, AL
    1956: Sarasota, FL
    1959: Casey Key, FL
    1960: Cambridge, MA
    1962: Tampa, FL
    1963: St. John's County, FL
    1965: Athens, AL
    1970: New York, NY
    1976: New York State
Rupp, William
    1960: Sarasota, FL
Salerno, Joseph
    1974: West Redding, CT
Salzman, Stanley
    1964: New York State
Sauer, Louis
    1967: Reston, VA
    1971: Margate, NJ
Schiffer, Joseph J.
    1965: Concord, MA
Schlesinger, Frank
    1961: Doylestown, PA
Schweitzer BIM
    1990: Joshua Tree, CA
Schwikher & Elting
    1956: Flossmoor, IL
Schwartz/Silver Architects
    1987: West Stockbridge, MA
Scogin Elam & Bray Architects
    1991: Atlanta, GA
Scott, J. Lawrence
    1977: Ohio
Seibert, Edward J.
    1961: Sarasota, FL
Sert, José Luis
    1959: Cambridge, MA
Sheine, Judith
    1995: Juniper Hills, CA
Sherwood, Mills & Smith
    1957: New Canaan, CT
Short, Sam B. & Ross G. Murrell
    1966: Baton Rouge, LA
Shope Reno Wharton Associates
    1987: Greenwich, CT
Sidnam, Caroline Northcote
    1984: Lancaster, PA
Siedel, Alexander & Jared Carlin
    1982: Napa, CA
Skolnick, Lee H.
    1990: Bridgehampton, NY
Simon, Mark
    1985: Eastern Long Island, NY

Singer, Donald
1969: Miami, FL
1971: Coconut Grove, FL
1975: Boca Raton, FL
1978: South Miami, FL
SITE Projects
1986: New York, NY
Slack, John
1979: Omaha, NE
Small & Boaz
1960: Raleigh, NC
Smith, Edgar Wilson
1965: Portland, OR
1967: Lake Oswego, OR
Smith, Joseph N.
1959: Miami, FL
Smith, & Larson
1973: Pebble Beach, CA
Smith-Miller + Hawkinson
1987: East Hampton, NY
1992: Los Angeles, CA
Smith, Melvin/Noel Yauch
1976: Massachusetts
Smith & Others
1985: San Diego, CA
1989: Coronado, CA
Smith & Williams
1956: Pasadena, CA
Smotrich & Platt
1971: Mendham, NJ
Sobel, Robert
1974: Houston, TX
Sorey, Thomas L., Jr.
1968: Oklahoma City, OK
Soriano, Raphael
1956: Bel Air, CA
Sottsass Studio & Maestrelli
1995: Tuscany, Italy

Specter, David Kenneth
1971: East Hampton, NY
Speyer, A. James
1956: Highland Park, IL
Stageberg, James Edgar
1962: Minneapolis, MN
1964: Chesterfield, MO
1968: Edina, MN
Stern, Robert A. M.
1981: Mt. Desert Island, ME
1984: East Hampton, NY
Strauss, Carl A.
1960: Cincinnati, OH
Strassman, Jim
1983: Peterborough, Ontario
Stubbins, Hugh
1959: Rhode Island
1967: Cambridge, MA
Teague, Harry
1982: Aspen, CO
Taft Architects
1985: Houston, TX
1991: Nevis, West Indies
Tanner Leddy Maytum Stacy Architects
1992: San Francisco, CA
1993: Kennett Square, PA
Taylor & Orr
1986: Seaside, FL
Ternstrom & Skinner
1965: South Pasadena, CA
Thiry, Paul
1956: Seattle, WA
1958: Seattle, WA
Tigerman/Fugman/McCurry
1987: Western Connecticut
Tigerman McCurry
1993: La Conchita, CA
Tigerman, Stanley & Associates
1980: Lisle, IL
Torre, Susana
1982: Eastern Long Island, NY

Torre, Beeler & Associates
1988: Amagansett, NY
Tremaglio, Richard C.
1985: Vineyard Haven, MA
Tilly, Stephen & Alan Buchsbaum
1983: Lexington, SC
Trout Architects
1978: Ohio
Twitchell & Miao
1974: New York State
Ungers, Simon & Tom Kinslow
1994: Wilton, NY
Valerio, Joseph & Linda Searl
1991: Chicago, IL
Vendensky, Dmitri
1975: Sea Ranch, CA
Venturi, Rauch and Scott Brown
1982: Block Island, RI
1984: Stony Creek, CT
1984: Wainscott, NY
Veronda Associates
1983: Buffalo, CA
Vise, Herbert
1967: York Harbor, ME
Wagener, Hobart D.
1967: Boulder, CO
Warner & Gray
1977: California
Warriner, Joan & Ken
1961: Sarasota, FL
Webb, Chard F.
1958: Phoenixville, PA
Webber, Elroy Associates
1962: South Hadley, MA
Weese, Harry
1960: Chicago, IL
1970: Canada
Weiner Gran Associates
1972: Westport, CT
Weisbach, Gerald G.
1968: Mill Valley, CA
West, J. & Associates
1965: Sarasota, FL
Wexler & Harrison
1963: Palm Springs, CA
Whisnant, Murray
1974: Charlotte, NC

Whitton, Robert
1974: Boxboro, MA
1981: Southern Florida
Wiener, Samuel G. & William B. & Associates
1956: Shreveport, LA
Wilkes, Joseph A. & Winthrop W. Faulkner
1968: McLean, VA
Williams, Gerald A.
1979: Seattle, WA
Wilson, Morris, Crain & Anderson
1969: Houston, TX
Wilson, Peter Associates
1982: Fire Island, NY
Woehle, Fritz
1964: Birmingham, AL
Woerner, Peter Kurt
1976: Guilford, CT
Wolf, Johnson & Associates
1970: North Carolina
Wong, Brocchini & Associates
1972: Santa Cruz, CA
Woo, George C. T.
1982: Qintana Roo, Mexico
Woo, Young
1967: Los Angeles, CA
Woollen, Evans III
1957: Indianapolis, IN
Wu, King-Lui
1966: Old Lyme, CT
1975: Killingsworth, CT
Wurster, Bernardi & Emmons
1956: Marin County, CA
Yamasaki, Leinweber & Associates
1957: Detroit, MI
Zapata, Carlos and Una Idea
1994: Golden Beach, FL
Zephyr Architectural Partnership
1980: Lanikai, HI

CREDITS

PAGE 1: COOPER HOUSE, 1970
CAPE COD, MASSACHUSETTS
GWATHMEY, HENDERSON, SIEGEL, ARCHITECTS
PHOTOGRAPH: BILL MARIS

PAGES 2–3: DENNISON/PEEK HOUSE, 1992
MONKTON, VERMONT
BROOKS & CAREY, ARCHITECTS
PHOTOGRAPH: © SCOTT FRANCES/ESTO

PAGES 4–5: TAFT HOUSE, 1981
CINCINNATI, OHIO
GWATHMEY SIEGEL, ARCHITECTS
PHOTOGRAPH: © RICHARD PAYNE

PAGES 6–7: LANDES HOUSE, 1994
GOLDEN BEACH, FLORIDA
CARLOS ZAPATA DESIGN STUDIO AND UNA IDEA,
ARCHITECTS
PHOTOGRAPH: © PETER AARON/ESTO

PAGE 8: T-HOUSE, 1994
WILTON, NEW YORK
SIMON UNGERS AND TOM KINSLOW, ARCHITECTS
PHOTOGRAPH: © ARCH PHOTO, INC./EDUARD
HUEBER

PAGES 8–11: CARTOONS © ALAN DUNN

PAGES 12–13: BEATTIE HOUSE, 1958
RYE, NEW YORK
ULRICH FRANZEN, ARCHITECT
PHOTOGRAPH: © EZRA STOLLER/ESTO

PAGES 14 AND 22–27: FRANZEN HOUSE, 1956
WESTCHESTER COUNTY, NEW YORK
ULRICH FRANZEN, ARCHITECT
PHOTOGRAPHS: © 1956 ELLIOTT ERWITT/MAGNUM
PHOTOS, INC. **(PAGE 14)**; © EZRA STOLLER/ESTO
(PAGES 23, 24, 26, 27)

PAGES 16–17 AND 28–29: COHEN HOUSE, 1956
SARASOTA, FLORIDA
PAUL RUDOLPH, ARCHITECT
PHOTOGRAPHS: © EZRA STOLLER/ESTO

PAGES 30–31: KIRKPATRICK HOUSE, 1958
KALAMAZOO, MICHIGAN
GEORGE NELSON AND GORDON CHADWICK,
ARCHITECTS
PHOTOGRAPHS: NORMAN F. CARVER, JR.

PAGES 32–35: BRIDGE HOUSE, 1958
FAIRFIELD, CONNECTICUT
JOHN MACL. JOHANSEN, ARCHITECT
PHOTOGRAPHS: ROBERT DAMORA

PAGES 36–37: GRAY HOUSE, 1958
OLYMPIA FIELDS, ILLINOIS
GEORGE FRED KECK AND WILLIAM KECK,
ARCHITECTS
PHOTOGRAPHS: BILL ENGDAHL/HEDRICH-BLESSING,
COURTESY CHICAGO HISTORICAL SOCIETY

PAGES 38–43: STARKEY HOUSE, 1958
DULUTH, MINNESOTA
MARCEL BREUER, ARCHITECT
HERBERT BECKHARD, ASSOCIATE
PHOTOGRAPHS: © EZRA STOLLER/ESTO

PAGES 44–47: SERT HOUSE, 1959
CAMBRIDGE, MASSACHUSETTS
JOSÉ LUIS SERT, ARCHITECT
PHOTOGRAPHS: JOHN SHEAHAN, COURTESY J. L.
SERT COLLECTION, FRANCES LOEB LIBRARY,
GRADUATE SCHOOL OF DESIGN, HARVARD
UNIVERSITY

PAGES 48–49: BECKWITH HOUSE, 1961
FRANKLIN HILLS, MICHIGAN
MEATHE, KESSLER & ASSOCIATES, ARCHITECTS
PHOTOGRAPH: BALTHAZAR KORAB LTD.

PAGE 50: FITZPATRICK HOUSE, 1969
YORKTOWN, NEW YORK
ROBERT FITZPATRICK, ARCHITECT
PHOTOGRAPH: JOSEPH W. MOLITOR

PAGES 54–55: FREEMAN RESIDENCE
(ATRIUM HOUSE), 1968
GRAND RAPIDS, MICHIGAN
GUNNAR BIRKERTS, ARCHITECT
PHOTOGRAPH: BILL ENGDAHL/HEDRICH-BLESSING

PAGE 57: JEROME MEIER HOUSE, 1964
ESSEX FALLS, NEW JERSEY
RICHARD MEIER, ARCHITECT
PHOTOGRAPH: © EZRA STOLLER/ESTO

PAGES 58–61: HOUSE NEAR ESSEX,
CONNECTICUT, 1960
ULRICH FRANZEN, ARCHITECT
PHOTOGRAPHS: ROBERT DAMORA

PAGES 62–63: HOOPER HOUSE, 1961
BALTIMORE, MARYLAND
MARCEL BREUER, ARCHITECT
HERBERT BECKHARD, ASSOCIATE
PHOTOGRAPHS: © WALTER SMALLING

PAGES 64–67: DEVELOPMENT HOUSE FOR
NEW SEABURY, 1962
CAPE COD, MASSACHUSETTS
ROBERT DAMORA, ARCHITECT
PHOTOGRAPHS: ROBERT DAMORA

PAGES 68–71: HOUSE ON LLOYD'S NECK,
1962
LONG ISLAND, NEW YORK
PHILIP JOHNSON, ARCHITECT
PHOTOGRAPHS: © EZRA STOLLER/ESTO

PAGES 72–73: BARROWS HOUSE, 1962
MARATHON SHORES, KEY VACA, FLORIDA
ROBERT B. BROWNE, ARCHITECT
G. F. REED, ASSOCIATE
PHOTOGRAPHS: JOSEPH W. MOLITOR

PAGES 74–75: HIRSCH HOUSE, 1963
HIGHLAND PARK, ILLINOIS
GEORGE FRED KECK AND WILLIAM KECK,
ARCHITECTS
PHOTOGRAPHS: BILL HEDRICH/HEDRICH-BLESSING
(PAGES 74 TOP AND 75); GIOVANNI SUTER/HEDRICH-
BLESSING **(PAGE 74 BOTTOM)**, COURTESY CHICAGO
HISTORICAL SOCIETY

PAGES 76–81: MILAM HOUSE, 1963
ST. JOHN'S COUNTY, FLORIDA
PAUL RUDOLPH, ARCHITECT
PHOTOGRAPHS: JOSEPH W. MOLITOR

PAGES 82–83: SLAYTON TOWNHOUSE, 1964
WASHINGTON, D.C.
I. M. PEI & ASSOCIATES, ARCHITECTS, WITH
KELLOGG WONG
PHOTOGRAPHS: ROBERT C. LAUTMAN **(PAGE 82)**;
JOSEPH W. MOLITOR **(PAGE 83)**

PAGES 84–89: BUNSHAFT HOUSE, 1966
EAST HAMPTON, NEW YORK
GORDON BUNSHAFT, ARCHITECT
PHOTOGRAPHS: © EZRA STOLLER/ESTO

PAGES 90–91: KARAS HOUSE, 1967
MONTEREY, CALIFORNIA
MLTW/MOORE-TURNBULL, ARCHITECTS
PHOTOGRAPHS: MORLEY BAER

PAGES 92–93: STRAUS HOUSE, 1968
PURCHASE, NEW YORK
GWATHMEY & HENDERSON, ARCHITECTS
PHOTOGRAPHS: BILL MARIS

PAGES 94–97: SMITH HOUSE, 1968
DARIEN, CONNECTICUT
RICHARD MEIER, ARCHITECT
PHOTOGRAPHS: © EZRA STOLLER/ESTO

PAGES 98–99: TRENTMAN HOUSE, 1969
WASHINGTON, D.C.
HUGH NEWELL JACOBSEN, ARCHITECT
PHOTOGRAPHS: ROBERT C. LAUTMAN

PAGES 100–01: BINKER BARN, 1973
SEA RANCH, CALIFORNIA
MLTW/MOORE-TURNBULL, ARCHITECTS
PHOTOGRAPHS: ARTHUR YOUNGMEISTER, COURTESY
WILLIAM TURNBULL ASSOCIATES

PAGES 102–03: APARTMENTS, 1973
TUSTIN, CALIFORNIA
BACKEN, ARRIGONI & ROSS, ARCHITECTS
PHOTOGRAPH: COURTESY BACKEN, ARRIGONI &
ROSS

PAGE 104: PRIVATE RESIDENCE, 1974
DARIEN, CONNECTICUT
HUYGENS AND TAPPÉ, ARCHITECTS
PHOTOGRAPH: JULIUS SHULMAN

PAGES 106–07: GRAHAM HOUSE, 1971
FAIRFIELD, CONNECTICUT
ELIOT NOYES, ARCHITECT
PHOTOGRAPH: JOSEPH W. MOLITOR

PAGE 109: WIERDSMA HOUSE, 1976
NANTUCKET, MASSACHUSETTS
LOUIS MACKALL, ARCHITECT
PHOTOGRAPH: © ROBERT PERRON

PAGE 111: COHEN HOUSE, 1978
SOUTH ORANGE, NEW JERSEY
BREUER AND BECKHARD, ARCHITECTS
PHOTOGRAPH: GIL AMIAGA

PAGES 112–15: HIRSCH/HALSTON
TOWNHOUSE, 1970
NEW YORK, NEW YORK
PAUL RUDOLPH, ARCHITECT
PHOTOGRAPHS: © EZRA STOLLER/ESTO

PAGES 116–19: LA LUZ TOWNHOUSES, 1970
ALBUQUERQUE, NEW MEXICO
ANTOINE PREDOCK, ARCHITECT
PHOTOGRAPHS: © TIMOTHY HURSLEY

PAGES 120–23: CONNECTICUT HOUSE, 1976
WEST CORNWALL, CONNECTICUT
BOHLIN AND POWELL, ARCHITECTS
PHOTOGRAPHS: JOSEPH W. MOLITOR

PAGES 124–25: HECKSCHER HOUSE, 1976
MT. DESERT ISLAND, MAINE
EDWARD LARRABEE BARNES, ARCHITECT
PHOTOGRAPHS: © DAVID FRANZEN/ESTO

PAGES 126–29: WOLF RESIDENCE, 1977
TORONTO, ONTARIO
BARTON MYERS, ARCHITECT
PHOTOGRAPHS: JOHN FULKER

PAGES 130–33: SHAMBERG HOUSE, 1977
WESTCHESTER, NEW YORK
RICHARD MEIER & ASSOCIATES, ARCHITECTS
PHOTOGRAPHS: © EZRA STOLLER/ESTO

PAGES 134–39: ARANGO HOUSE, 1977
ACAPULCO, MEXICO
JOHN LAUTNER, ARCHITECT
PHOTOGRAPHS: © MIKE MOORE

PAGES 140–41: KRIEGER HOUSE, 1977
EASTERN LONG ISLAND, NEW YORK
NORMAN JAFFE, ARCHITECT
PHOTOGRAPHS: BILL MARIS

PAGES 142–43: HOUSE IN THE SANDIA
MOUNTAINS, 1977
ALBUQUERQUE, NEW MEXICO
ANTOINE PREDOCK, ARCHITECT
PHOTOGRAPHS: JOSHUA FREILAND

PAGES 144–47: HULSE HOUSE, 1978
ATLANTA, GEORGIA
ANTHONY AMES, ARCHITECT
PHOTOGRAPHS: E. ALAN MCGEE

PAGES 148–49: BARN ON THE CHOPTANK,
1978
EASTERN SHORE, MARYLAND
MOORE GROVER HARPER, ARCHITECTS
PHOTOGRAPHS: NORMAN MCGRATH

PAGES 150–51: PALLONE HOUSE, 1978
CENTRAL ARKANSAS
E. FAY JONES, ARCHITECT
PHOTOGRAPHS: RICHARD PAYNE

PAGES 152–55: HAUPT HOUSE, 1979
AMAGANSETT, NEW YORK
GWATHMEY SIEGEL, ARCHITECTS
PHOTOGRAPHS: NORMAN MCGRATH

PAGES 156–57: HOLLYWOOD DUPLEX, 1988
LOS ANGELES, CALIFORNIA
KONING EIZENBERG ARCHITECTURE
PHOTOGRAPH: TIM STREET-PORTER

PAGES 158–59: IZENOUR HOUSE, 1984
STONY CREEK, CONNECTICUT
VENTURI, RAUCH AND SCOTT BROWN,
ARCHITECTS
PHOTOGRAPH: TOM BERNARD

PAGE 161: GAFFNEY HOUSE, 1981
ROMANSVILLE, PENNSYLVANIA
BOHLIN POWELL LARKIN & CYWINSKI,
ARCHITECTS
PHOTOGRAPH: JOSEPH W. MOLITOR

PAGE 162: MARTIN HOUSE, 1993
KENNETT SQUARE, PENNSYLVANIA
TANNER LEDDY MAYTUM STACY, ARCHITECTS
PHOTOGRAPH: © PAUL WARCHOL

PAGES 164–65: DRAGER HOUSE, 1995
OAKLAND, CALIFORNIA
FRANKLIN D. ISRAEL DESIGN, ARCHITECTS
PHOTOGRAPH: © GRANT MUDFORD

PAGES 166–67: WRIGHT GUEST HOUSE,
1989
SEATTLE, WASHINGTON
JAMES CUTLER, ARCHITECT
PHOTOGRAPH: © PETER AARON/ESTO

PAGES 168–71: COXE-HAYDEN HOUSE AND
STUDIO, 1982
BLOCK ISLAND, RHODE ISLAND
VENTURI, RAUCH AND SCOTT BROWN,
ARCHITECTS
PHOTOGRAPHS: TOM BERNARD

PAGES 172–75: HOG HILL HOUSE, 1983
EAST HOLDEN, MAINE
BENTLEY/LAROSA/SALASKY DESIGN,
ARCHITECTS
PHOTOGRAPHS: © TIMOTHY HURSLEY

PAGES 176–77: HIBISCUS HOUSE, 1983
COCONUT GROVE, FLORIDA
ANDRES DUANY AND ELIZABETH PLATER-
ZYBERK, ARCHITECTS
PHOTOGRAPHS: STEVEN BROOKE

PAGES 178–81: SPILLER HOUSES, 1983
VENICE, CALIFORNIA
FRANK O. GEHRY & ASSOCIATES, ARCHITECTS
PHOTOGRAPHS: © TIM STREET-PORTER/ESTO

PAGES 182–85: HOUSE ON LAKE
MEMPHREMAGOG, 1984
AUSTIN, QUEBEC
PETER ROSE, ARCHITECT
PHOTOGRAPHS: © TIMOTHY HURSLEY

PAGES 186–89: VILLA ON THE BAY, 1984
CORPUS CHRISTI, TEXAS
BATEY & MACK, ARCHITECTS
PHOTOGRAPHS: © TIM STREET-PORTER

PAGES 190–91: PRIVATE HOUSE, 1984
NORTHEASTERN COAST
GRAHAM GUND ASSOCIATES, ARCHITECTS
PHOTOGRAPHS: © STEVE ROSENTHAL

PAGES 192–97: NORTON HOUSE, 1985
VENICE, CALIFORNIA
FRANK O. GEHRY AND ASSOCIATES, ARCHITECTS
PHOTOGRAPHS: © TIM STREET-PORTER/ESTO **(PAGES
195, 197 BOTTOM);** © TIMOTHY HURSLEY **(PAGES
192–94, 196, 197 TOP)**

PAGES 198–201: PRINCE HOUSE, 1985
ALBUQUERQUE, NEW MEXICO
BART PRINCE, ARCHITECT
PHOTOGRAPHS: © ROBERT RECK

PAGES 202–05: CASA LOS ANDES, 1986
LIMA, PERU
ARQUITECTONICA INTERNATIONAL
CORPORATION, ARCHITECT
PHOTOGRAPHS: © TIMOTHY HURSLEY

PAGES 206–11: FARMHOUSE IN
CONNECTICUT, 1986
ALLAN GREENBERG, ARCHITECT
PHOTOGRAPHS: © PETER MAUSS/ESTO

PAGES 212–17: BERGGRUEN HOUSE, 1989
RUTHERFORD, CALIFORNIA
FERNAU AND HARTMAN, ARCHITECTS
PHOTOGRAPHS: © CHRISTOPHER IRION

PAGES 218–21: THE MONUMENT, 1990
JOSHUA TREE, CALIFORNIA
SCHWEITZER BIM, ARCHITECT
PHOTOGRAPHS: © TIMOTHY HURSLEY

PAGES 222–27: CHMAR HOUSE, 1991
ATLANTA, GEORGIA
SCOGIN ELAM AND BRAY, ARCHITECTS
PHOTOGRAPHS: © TIMOTHY HURSLEY

PAGE 239: BUCKWALTER HOUSE, 1981
CENTRAL PENNSYLVANIA
HUGH NEWELL JACOBSEN, ARCHITECT
PHOTOGRAPH: ROBERT C. LAUTMAN

INDEX

Page numbers in *italics* refer to illustrations.

Acapulco, Mexico
  Arango House, 108, 134–36, *134, 135, 136, 137,*
    138, 139
Alabama
  Applebee House, *20, 21*
Albers, Joseph, 25
Albuquerque, N.M.
  House in the Sandia Mountains, 110, 142–
    43, *142, 143*
  La Luz Townhouses, 110, 116–17, *116, 117,*
    118–19
  Prince House, 198–201, *198, 199, 200, 201*
Amagansett, N.Y.
  Haupt House, 152–53, *152, 153, 154, 155*
Ames, Anthony
  Hulse House, 108, 144–45, *144, 145, 146–47*
Apartments, 160
  by Backen, Arrigoni & Ross, *102*
Applebee House, *20, 21*
Arango House, 108, 134–36, *134, 135, 136, 137,*
    138, 139
Architectural Record, 8
  See also Record Houses
Architectural schools, 24–25, 51–52, 105
Arkansas
  Pallone House, 105, 150–51, *150, 151*
Arquitectonica International Corporation
  Casa Los Andes, 202–5, *202, 203, 204, 205*
Asplund, Gunnar, 110
Atlanta, Ga.
  Chmar House, 167, 222–26, *222, 223, 224,*
    225, 226, 227
  Hulse House, 108, 144–45, *144, 145,*
    146–47
Atrium House (Freeman residence), *54–55*
Auburn, Ala.
  Applebee House, *20, 21*
Austin, Quebec
  House on Lake Memphremagog, 182–85,
    182, 183, 184, 185

Backen, Arrigoni & Ross
  Apartments, *102*
Baltimore, Md.
  Hooper House, 53, 62, *62, 63*
Barnes, Edward Larrabee, 105, 106
  Heckscher House, 105, 124–25, *124, 125*
Barn on the Choptank, 110, 148, *148, 149*
Baroque style, 207
Barragan, Luis, 218–19
Barrows House, 53, 72–73, *72, 73*
Batey & Mack
  Villa on the Bay, 163, 186–87, *186, 187,*
    188, 189
Bauhaus, 24, 25, 51, 53, 105, 108, 176
Bayer, Herbert, 25

Beattie House, *12–13*
Beckhard, Herbert, *38, 62*
  Cohen House, *111*
Beckwith House, *48–49*
Bentley, Ronald, 172
Bentley/LaRosa/Salasky Design, 163
  Hog Hill House, 163, 172–75, *172, 173,*
    174, 175
Berggruen House, 212–13, *212, 213, 214–15,*
    216, 217
Binker Barn, 11, *100–01, 102,* 110
Birkerts, Gunnar
  Freeman residence (Atrium House), *54–55*
Blake, Peter, 52
Block Island, R.I.
  Coxe–Hayden House and Studio, 168–69,
    168, 169, 170–71
Bohlin and Powell
  Connecticut House, 106, 120–22, *120, 121,*
    122, 123
Bohlin Powell Larkin & Cywinski
  Gaffney House, 160, *160, 161*
Botta, Mario, 163
Bray, Lloyd
  Chmar House, 167, 222–26, *222, 223, 224,*
    225, 226, 227
Brenner, Douglas, 10–11
Breuer, Marcel, 25, 53, 105, 108
  Cohen House, *111*
  Hooper House, 53, 62, *62, 63*
  Starkey House, 38–39, *38, 39, 40, 41,*
    42, 43
Bridge House, 32–33, *32, 33, 34, 35*
Brooks & Carey
  Dennison/Peek House, *2–3*
Brown, Denise Scott, 103
Browne, Robert B.
  Barrows House, 53, 72–73, *72, 73*
Buckwalter House, *239*
Bunshaft, Gordon
  Bunshaft House, 56, 84–89, *84–85, 86–87,*
    88, 89

California
  apartments, *102*
  Berggruen House, 212–13, *212, 213, 214–15,*
    216, 217
  Binker Barn, 11, *100–101, 102,* 110
  Drager House, *164–65,* 167
  Hollywood Duplex, *156–57, 159,* 167
  Karas House, 11, 56, 90, *90, 91*
  The Monument, 167, 218–20, *218, 219,*
    220, 221
  Norton House, 11, 192–97, *192, 193, 194, 195,*
    196, 197
  Spiller Houses, 11, 178–81, *178–79,*
    180, 181
Cambridge, Mass.
  Sert House, 17, 44–47, *44, 45, 46, 47*

Campbell, Robert, 51–56
Canada
  House on Lake Memphremagog, 182–85,
    182, 183, 184, 185
  Wolf House, 106, 126–29, *126, 127, 128, 129*
Cape Cod, Mass.
  Cooper House, *1*
  Development House for New Seabury, 52,
    53, 64–67, *64, 65, 66, 67*
Carlos Zapata Design Studio
  Landes House, *6–7*
Casa Los Andes, 202–5, *202, 203, 204, 205*
Centre Pompidou, 105–6
Chadwick, Gordon
  Kirkpatrick House, 15, 30–31, *30, 31*
Chimacoff, Alan
  Lowenstein House, 108
Chmar House, 167, 222–26, *222, 223, 224, 225,*
    226, 227
Choptank River, Barn on, 110, 148, *148, 149*
Cincinnati, Oh.
  Taft House, *4–5*
Classicism, 206, 207, 210, 211
Cobb, Harry, 105
Coconut Grove, Fla.
  Hibiscus House, 176–77, *176, 177*
Cohen House (Breuer and Beckhard), *111*
Cohen House (Rudolph), *16–17,* 28, *28, 29*
Colonial style, 207, 211
Complexity and Contradiction in Architecture
  (Venturi), 51
Connecticut
  Bridge House, 32–33, *32, 33, 34, 35*
  Connecticut House, 106, 120–22, *120, 121,*
    122, 123
  Farmhouse, 9, 206–11, *206, 207, 208, 209,*
    210, 211
  Graham House, *106–7*
  House near Essex, 58–59, *58, 59,*
    60–61
  Izenour House, *158–59*
  private residence, *104*
  Smith House, 56, 94, *94, 95, 96–97*
Conversation pit, 53
Cooper House, *1*
Corpus Christi, Tex.
  Villa on the Bay, 163, 186–87, *186, 187,*
    188, 189
Coxe–Hayden House and Studio, 168–69, *168,*
    169, 170–71
Culture of Narcissism, The: American Life in
  an Age of Diminishing Expectations
  (Lasch), 110
Curtain walls, 36–37
Cutler, James
  Wright Guest House, *166–67*

Damora, Robert
  Development House for New Seabury, 52,
    53, 64–67, *64, 65, 66, 67*
Darien, Conn.
  private residence, *104*
  Smith House, 56, 94, *94, 95, 96–97*
Deamer, Peggy, 108
Dearstyne, Howard, 25
Decorated Diagram, The: Harvard
  Architecture and the Failure of the
  Bauhaus Legacy (Herdeg), 106
Dennison/Peek House, *2–3*
Depression, Great, 19, 24
Development House for New Seabury, 52, 53,
    64–67, *64, 65, 66, 67*
Dimella Shaffer Associates (Huygens and
    Tappé Inc.)
  private residence, *104,* 110
Drager House, *164–65,* 167
Duany, Andres, 176
  Hibiscus House, 176–77, *176, 177*
Duluth, Minn.
  Starkey House, 38–39, *38, 39, 40, 41, 42, 43*

Earl, Harley, 19
East Hampton, N.Y.
  Bunshaft House, 56, 84–89, *84–85, 86–87,*
    88, 89
East Holden, Me.
  Hog Hill House, 163, 172–75, *172, 173,*
    174, 175
Eisenman, Peter, 103, 160
Eisenman/Robertson, 160
Elam, Merrill
  Chmar House, 167, 222–26, *222, 223, 224,*
    225, 226, 227
Ellwood, Craig, 15–17, 56
Engman, Robert, 33
Erwitt, Elliott, 9, 15, *15,* 17
Essex, Conn.
  House near, 58–59, *58, 59, 60–61*
Essex Falls, N.J.
  Jerome Meier House, *57*

Fairfield, Conn.
  Bridge House, 32–33, *32, 33, 34, 35*
  Graham House, *106–7*
  Farmhouse in Connecticut, 9, 206–11, *206,*
    207, 208, 209, 210, 211
Fences, 17, 47
  See also Walled courts
Fernau, Richard
  Berggruen House, 212–13, *212, 213, 214–15,*
    216, 217
Ferri, Roger, 163
Fitzpatrick, Robert
  Fitzpatrick House, *50, 51*

Florida
  Barrows House, 53, 72–73, *72, 73*
  Cohen House, *16–17,* 28, *28, 29*
  Hibiscus House, 176–77, *176, 177*
  Landes House, *6–7*
  Milam House, 53–56, 76–79, *76, 77, 78, 79, 80, 81*
Formalism, 106–08
Fort-Brescia, Bernardo, 160
Franklin D. Israel Design
  Drager House, *164–65,* 167
Franklin Hills, Mich.
  Beckwith House, *48–49*
Franzen, Ulrich, 18, 22, 105
  Beattie House, *12–13*
  Franzen House, 9, 10, 15, *14, 15,* 18–19, 21, 22, *22, 23,* 26, 27, 52–53, 58
  House Near Essex, Connecticut, 58–59, *58, 59, 60–61*
Freeman residence (Atrium House), *54–55*
Furniture, 28, 47, 53, 209
  butterfly chairs, 21

Gaffney House, 160, *160, 161*
Gandee, Charles, 159–67
Gauguin, Paul, 22
Gehry, Frank O., 53, 103, 160, *160,* 219
  Norton House, 11, 192–97, *192, 193, 194, 195, 196, 197*
  Spiller Houses, 11, 178–81, *178–79, 180, 181*
Georgia
  Chmar House, 167, 222–26, *222, 223, 224, 225, 226, 227*
  Hulse House, 108, 144–45, *144, 145, 146–47*
Goff, Bruce, 198, 200
Golden Beach, Fla.
  Landes House, *6–7*
Gonzales, Bennie, 53
Gordon, Barclay, 10
Graham Gund Associates
  House on the Northeastern Coast, 190, *190, 191*
Graham House, *106–7*
Grand Rapids, Mich.
  Freeman residence (Atrium House), *54–55*
Graves, Michael, 103, 160, 163
Gray House, 36–37, *36, 37*
Greenberg, Allan
  Farmhouse in Connecticut, 9, 206–11, *206, 207, 208, 209, 210, 211*
Gregory, Jules, 53
Gropius, Walter, 10, 15, 24–25, 105, 108
Guild House, 51
Gwathmey, Charles, 56
Gwathmey, Henderson, Siegel, 108
  Cooper House, *1*
Gwathmey & Henderson
  Straus House, 92, *92, 93*
Gwathmey Siegel & Associates, 9, 163
  Haupt House, 152–53, *152, 153, 154, 155*
  Taft House, *4–5*

Halston, 105
Hammond Beeby and Babka, 160
Hartman, Laura
  Berggruen House, 212–13, *212, 213, 214–15, 216, 217*
Haupt House, 152–53, *152, 153, 154, 155*
Heckscher House, 105, 124–25, *124, 125*
Herdeg, Klaus, 106
Hibiscus House, 176–77, *176, 177*
Highland Park, Ill.
  Hirsch House, 74–75, *74, 75*
Hine, Thomas, 15–21
Hirsch House, 74–75, *74, 75*
Hirsch/Halston Townhouse, 105, 112–15, *112, 113, 114, 115*
Historic buildings, preservation of, 110
Historicism, 103, 110
Hog Hill House, 163, 172–75, *172, 173, 174, 175*
Holl, Steven, 160
Hollywood Duplex, *156–57, 159,* 167
Hooper House, 53, 62, *62, 63*
House in the Sandia Mountains, 110, 142–43, *142, 143*
House Near Essex, Connecticut, 58–59, *58, 59, 60–61*
House on Lake Memphremagog, 182–85, *182, 183, 184, 185*
House on Lloyd's Neck, 56, 68–69, *68, 69, 70, 71*
House on the Northeastern Coast, 190, *190, 191*
Housing developments, 19
  Development House for New Seabury, 52, 53, 64–67, *64, 65, 66, 67*
Hulse House, 108, 144–45, *144, 145, 146–47*
Huygens and Tappé Inc. (Dimella Shaffer Associates)
  private residence, *104,* 110

IBM Tower, 105
Illinois
  Gray House, 36–37, *36, 37*
  Hirsch House, 74–75, *74, 75*
Industrial design, residential design vs., 126
Insecticides, 18, 27
International Style, 51
Israel, Franklin D.
  Drager House, *164–65,* 167
Izenour House, *158–59*

Jacobsen, Hugh Newell, 159, 160, 163
  Buckwalter House, *239*
  Trentman House, 56, 98, *98, 99*
Jaffe, Norman, 106–8
  Krieger House, 108, 140–41, *140, 141*
Jerome Meier House, *57*
Johansen, John MacL., 105
  Bridge House, 32–33, *32, 33, 34, 35*
Johnson, Philip, 105
  House on Lloyd's Neck, 56, 68–69, *68, 69, 70, 71*
Jones, E. Fay
  Pallone House, 105, 150–51, *150, 151*
Joshua Tree, Calif.
  The Monument, 167, 218–20, *218, 219, 220, 221*

Kahn, Louis, 150
Kalamazoo, Mich.
  Kirkpatrick House, 15, 30–31, *30, 31*
Karas House, 11, 56, 90, *90, 91*
Keck, George Fred and William
  Gray House, 36–37, *36, 37*
  Hirsch House, 74–75, *74, 75*
Kennett Square, Pa.
  Martin House, *162*
Key Vaca, Fla.
  Barrows House, 53, 72–73, *72, 73*
Kinslow, Tom
  T-House, *8*
Kirkpatrick House, 15, 30–31, *30, 31*
Kocher, A. Lawrence, 15, 18, 19, 22–27
Koning Eizenberg Architecture
  Hollywood Duplex, *156–57, 159,* 167
Koolhaas, Rem, 160, 163
Korab, Balthazar, 53
Krieger House, 108, 140–41, *140, 141*

Ladd & Kelsey, 53
Lake Memphremagog, House on, 182–85, *182, 183, 184, 185*
La Luz Townhouses, 110, 116–17, *116, 117, 118–19*
Landes House, *6–7*
Landmark buildings, 110
Lasch, Christopher, 110
Lautner, John, 108
  Arango House, 108, 134–36, *134, 135, 136, 137, 138, 139*
Le Corbusier, 52, 56, 105, 108
Levitt, William, 8
Lighting, 31
Lima, Peru
  Casa Los Andes, 202–5, *202, 203, 204, 205*
Lloyd's Neck, House on, 56, 68–69, *68, 69, 70, 71*
Long Island, N.Y.
  House on Lloyd's Neck, 56, 68–69, *68, 69, 70, 71*
  Krieger House, 108, 140–41, *140, 141*
Loos, Adolf, 51
Los Angeles, Calif.
  Hollywood Duplex, *156–57, 159,* 167
Lowenstein House, 108
Lutyens, Edwin Landseer, 208
Lynes, Russell, 21

Machado, Rodolfo, 160
Mack, Mark. *See* Batey & Mack
Mackall, Louis
  Wierdsma House, *109*
Maine
  Heckscher House, 105, 124–25, *124, 125*
  Hog Hill House, 163, 172–75, *172, 173, 174, 175*
Maisons Jaoul, 56
Martin House, *162*
Maryland
  Barn on the Choptank, 110, 148, *148, 149*
  Hooper House, 53, 62, *62, 63*

Massachusetts
  Cooper House, *1*
  Development House for New Seabury, 52, 53, 64–67, *64, 65, 66, 67*
  Sert House, 17, 44–47, *44, 45, 46, 47*
  Wierdsma House, *109*
Master Builders, The (Blake), 52
Meathe, Kessler & Associates
  Beckwith House, *48–49*
Meier, Richard, 56, 108
  Jerome Meier House, *57*
  Shamberg House, 108, 130–31, *130, 131, 132, 133*
  Smith House, 56, 94, *94, 95, 96–97*
Mexico
  Arango House, 108, 134–36, *134, 135, 136, 137, 138, 139*
Michigan
  Beckwith House, *48–49*
  Freeman residence (Atrium House), *54–55*
  Kirkpatrick House, 15, 30–31, *30, 31*
Mies van der Rohe, Ludwig, 10, 25, 26, 52, 56, 69, 105, 108, 160, 206
Milam House, 53–56, 76–79, *76, 77, 78, 79, 80, 81*
Minnesota
  Starkey House, 38–39, *38, 39, 40, 41, 42, 43*
MLTW/Moore-Turnbull
  Binker Barn, 11, *100–01, 102,* 110
  Karas House, 11, 56, 90, *90, 91*
  Sea Ranch, 110
Modernism, 9, 11, 15, 17, 18, 51, 103–5, 106, 110
  formalism and, 106–8
  heating and cooling costs and, 108
  historicism and, 103, 110
  regional traditions combined with, 53, 72, 108–10
Moholy-Nagy, L., 25
Monkton, Vt.
  Dennison/Peek House, *2–3*
Monterey, Calif.
  Karas House, 11, 56, 90, *90, 91*
Monument, The, 167, 218–20, *218, 219, 220, 221*
Moore, Charles, 103
  Binker Barn, 11, *100–01, 102,* 110
  Karas House, 11, 56, 90, *90, 91*
Moore Grover Harper
  Barn on the Choptank, 110, 148, *148, 149*
Morgan, William, 160
Moss, Eric Owen, 11
Mount Desert Island, Maine
  Heckscher House, 105, 124–25, *124, 125*
Mount Vernon, 206
Mumford, Lewis, 26
Myers, Barton
  Wolf House, 106, 126–29, *126, 127, 128, 129*

Nantucket, Mass.
  Wierdsma House, *109*
Nelson, George
  Kirkpatrick House, 15, 30–31, *30, 31*
New Jersey
  Cohen House, *111*
  Jerome Meier House, *57*

New Mexico
    House in the Sandia Mountains, 110,
      142–43, *142, 143*
    La Luz Townhouses, 110, 116–17, *116, 117,*
      118–19
    Prince House, 198–201, *198, 199, 200, 201*
New Primitivism, 220
New Seabury, Development House for, 52, 53,
    64–67, *64, 65, 66, 67*
New York
    Beattie House, *12–13*
    Bunshaft House, 56, 84–89, *84–85, 86–87,*
      88, 89
    Fitzpatrick House, *50, 51*
    Franzen House, 9, 10, 15, *14, 15,* 18–19, 21,
      22, *22, 23,* 26, 27, 52–53, 58
    Haupt House, 152–53, *152, 153, 154, 155*
    Hirsch/Halston Townhouse, 105, 112–15, *112,*
      113, 114, 115
    House on Lloyd's Neck, 56, 68–69, *68, 69,*
      70, 71
    Krieger House, 108, 140–41, *140, 141*
    Shamberg House, 108, 130–31, *130, 131,*
      132, 133
    Straus House, 92, *92, 93*
    T-House, *8*
1950s, 12–47
    Bridge House, 32–33, *32, 33, 34, 35*
    Cohen House, *16–17,* 28, *28, 29*
    Gray House, 36–37, *36, 37*
    Kirkpatrick House, 15, 30–31, *30, 31*
    Sert House, 17, 44–47, *44, 45, 46, 47*
    Starkey House, 38–39, *38, 39, 40, 41,*
      42, 43
1960s, 48–99
    Barrows House, 53, 72–73, *72, 73*
    Bunshaft House, 56, 84–89, *84–85, 86–87,*
      88, 89
    Development House for New Seabury, 52,
      53, 64–67, *64, 65, 66, 67*
    Hirsch House, 74–75, *74, 75*
    Hooper House, 53, 62, *62, 63*
    House Near Essex, Connecticut,
      58–59, *58, 59, 60–61*
    House on Lloyd's Neck, 56, 68–69, *68, 69,*
      70, 71
    Karas House, 11, 56, 90, *90, 91*
    Milam House, 53–56, 76–79, *76,*
      77, 78, 79, 80, 81
    Slayton Townhouse, 56, 82–83, *82, 83*
    Smith House, 56, 94, *94, 95, 96–97*
    Straus House, 92, *92, 93*
    Trentman House, 56, 98, *98, 99*
1970s, 101–55
    Arango House, 108, 134–36, *134, 135, 136,*
      137, 138, 139
    Barn on the Choptank, 110, 148, *148, 149*
    Connecticut House, 106, 120–22, *120, 121,*
      122, 123
    Haupt House, 152–53, *152, 153, 154, 155*
    Heckscher House, 105, 124–25, *124, 125*
    Hirsch/Halston Townhouse, 105, 112–15, *112,*
      113, 114, 115

House in the Sandia Mountains, 110, 142–
    43, *142, 143*
Hulse House, 108, 144–45, *144, 145, 146–47*
Krieger House, 108, 140–41, *140, 141*
La Luz Townhouses, 110, 116–17, *116, 117,*
    118–19
Pallone House, 105, 150–51, *150, 151*
Shamberg House, 108, 130–31, *130, 131,*
    132, 133
Wolf House, 106, 126–29, *126, 127, 128, 129*
1980s and 1990s, 157–227
    Berggruen House, 212–13, *212, 213, 214–15,*
      216, 217
    Casa Los Andes, 202–5, *202, 203, 204, 205*
    Chmar House, 167, 222–26, *222, 223, 224,*
      225, 226, 227
    Coxe-Hayden House and Studio, 168–69,
      168, 169, 170–71
    Farmhouse in Connecticut, 9, 206–11, *206,*
      207, 208, 209, 210, 211
    Hibiscus House, 176–77, *176, 177*
    Hog Hill House, 163, 172–75, *172, 173, 174, 175*
    House on Lake Memphremagog, 182–85,
      182, 183, 184, 185
    House on the Northeastern Coast, 190,
      190, 191
    The Monument, 167, 218–20, *218, 219, 220, 221*
    Norton House, 11, 192–97, *192, 193, 194, 195,*
      196, 197
    Prince House, 198–201, *198, 199, 200, 201*
    Spiller Houses, 11, 178–81, *178–79, 180, 181*
    Villa on the Bay, 163, 186–87, *186, 187,*
      188, 189
Northeastern Coast, House on, 190, *190, 191*
Norton House, 11, 192–97, *192, 193, 194, 195,*
    196, 197
Noyes, Eliot
    Graham House, *106–7*

Oakland, Calif.
    Drager House, *164–65,* 167
Ohio
    Taft House, *4–5*
Olympia Fields, Ill.
    Gray House, 36–37, *36, 37*
Ontario
    Wolf House, 106, 126–29, *126, 127, 128, 129*
Open plan, 15, 18, 19
Ornament, 19, 51, 53

Pallone House, 105, 150–51, *150, 151*
Patio house, 44–47
Pearson, Clifford A., 8–11
Pei, I. M., 105
    Slayton Townhouse, 56, 82–83, *82, 83*
Pennsylvania
    Buckwalter House, *239*
    Gaffney House, 160, *160, 161*
    Martin House, *162*
Perret, August, 26
Peru
    Casa Los Andes, 202–5, *202, 203, 204, 205*
Peterson, Steven
    Lowenstein House, 108

Photography, change from black-and-white to
    color, 56
Piano, Renzo, 105
Plater-Zyberk, Elizabeth, 176
    Hibiscus House, 176–77, *176, 177*
Postmodernism, 51, 56, 103, 110, 206
Predock, Antoine, 108–10
    House in the Sandia Mountains, 110,
      142–43, *142, 143*
    La Luz Townhouses, 110, 116–17, *116, 117,*
      118–19
Prefabricated houses. *See* Housing
    developments
Prince, Bart
    Prince House, 198–201, *198, 199, 200, 201*
Progressive Architecture, 160
Purchase, N.Y.
    Straus House, 92, *92, 93*

Quebec
    House on Lake Memphremagog, 182–85,
      182, 183, 184, 185

Record Houses, 8–11
    old-boy network and, 159–63
    Progressive Architecture and, 160
    redesign of, 163
Reed, G. F., 72
Regionalism, 53, 72, 108–10, 116, 125, 143, 163,
    168, 180–81, 201, 212
Renovations, 110
    Barn on the Choptank, 110, 148, *148, 149*
Rhode Island
    Coxe-Hayden House and Studio, 168–69,
      168, 169, 170–71
Rogers, Richard, 105
Romansville, Pa.
    Gaffney House, 160, *160, 161*
Romney, George, 52
Roofs, 18–19, 190
Rose, Peter
    House on Lake Memphremagog, 182–85,
      182, 183, 184, 185
Rossi, Aldo, 160–63
Rudolph, Paul, 56, 105, 106
    Applebee House, *20, 21*
    Cohen House, *16–17,* 28, *28, 29*
    Hirsch/Halston Townhouse, 105, 112–15, *112,*
      113, 114, 115
    Milam House, 53–56, 76–79, *76, 77, 78, 79,*
      80, 81
Rutherford, Calif.
    Berggruen House, 212–13, *212, 213, 214–15,*
      216, 217
Rye, N.Y.
    Beattie House, *12–13*

St. John's County, Fla.
    Milam House, 53–56, 76–79, *76, 77, 78, 79,*
      80, 81
Sandia Mountains, House in, 110, 142–43,
    142, 143
Sarasota, Fla.
    Cohen House, *16–17,* 28, *28, 29*

Schools, architectural, 24–25, 51–52, 105
Schweitzer, Josh
    The Monument, 167, 218–20, *218, 219, 220, 221*
Scogin, Mack
    Chmar House, 167, 222–26, *222, 223, 224,*
      225, 226, 227
Screens, 18, 27, 72–73
Sea Ranch, Calif.
    Binker Barn, 11, *100–101, 102,* 110
Seattle, Wash.
    Wright Guest House, *166–67*
Sert, José Luis, 44
    Sert House, 17, 44–47, *44, 45, 46, 47*
Shamberg House, 108, 130–31, *130, 131, 132, 133*
Shaw, George Bernard, 24
Silvetti, Jorge, 160
Size of houses, 21
Slayton Townhouse, 56, 82–83, *82, 83*
Smith, Herbert L., Jr., 9, 10
Smith House, 56, 94, *94, 95, 96–97*
Solar collectors, 143, 148
South America
    Casa Los Andes, 202–5, *202, 203, 204, 205*
South Orange, N.J.
    Cohen House, *111*
Spear, Laurinda, 160
Spielberg, Steven, 9
Spiller Houses, 11, 178–81, *178–79, 180, 181*
Starkey House, 38–39, *38, 39, 40, 41, 42, 43*
Stein, Karen, 8, 10
Stephens, Suzanne, 103–10
Stern, Robert A. M., 11, 103, 160, 163
Stoller, Ezra, 18, 51
Stone, Edward Durrell, 19
Stony Creek, Conn.
    Izenour House, *158–59*
Straus House, 92, *92, 93*
Suburbs, 18
Sullivan, Louis, 198, 200
Sun scoop, 90

Taft House, *4–5*
Tailfins, 18, 19
Tanner Leddy Maytum Stacy
    Martin House, *162*
Teague, Harry, 163
Texas
    Villa on the Bay, 163, 186–87, *186, 187,*
      188, 189
T-House, *8*
Tigerman, Stanley, 103
Toronto, Ontario
    Wolf House, 106, 126–29, *126, 127, 128, 129*
Torre, Susana, 163
Townhouses
    Hirsch/Halston, 105, 112–15, *112, 113,*
      114, 115
    La Luz, 110, 116–17, *116, 117, 118–19*
    Trentman, 56, 98, *98, 99*
    Trentman House, 56, 98, *98, 99*
Turnbull, William
    Binker Barn, 11, *100–101, 102,* 110
    Karas House, 11, 56, 90, *90, 91*

BUCKWALTER HOUSE
CENTRAL PENNSYLVANIA
HUGH NEWELL JACOBSEN, ARCHITECT
1981

Tustin, Calif.
    apartments in, *102*

Una Idea
    Landes House, *7*
Ungers, Simon
    T-House, *8*

Valerio, Joseph, 11
Vanna Venturi House, 56
Venice, Calif.
    Norton House, 11, 192–97, *192, 193, 194, 195,*
    196, 197
    Spiller Houses, 11, *178–81, 178–79, 180, 181*
Venturi, Robert, 11, 103, 160, 209
    Complexity and Contradiction in
    Architecture, 51
    Vanna Venturi House, 56
Venturi, Rauch and Scott Brown, 160, 163
    Coxe-Hayden House and Studio, 168–69,
    168, 169, 170–71
    Izenour House, *158–59*
Vermont
    Dennison/Peek House, *2–3*
Vignelli, Massimo, 163
Villa on the Bay, 163, 186–87, *186, 187, 188, 189*
Voysey, C. F. A., 110

Wagner, Walter, 159
Walker Art Center, 105
Walled courts, 17, 202, 205
    patio house, 44–47
Walls, 25–26
Washington
    Wright Guest House, *166–67*
Washington, D.C.
    Slayton Townhouse, 56, 82–83, *82, 83*
    Trentman House, 56, 98, *98, 99*
Westchester, N.Y.
    Franzen House, 9, 10, 15, *14, 15,* 18–19, 21,
    22, *22, 23,* 26, 27, 52–53, 58
    Shamberg House, 108, 130–31, *130, 131,*
    132, 133
West Cornwall, Conn.
    Connecticut House, 106, 120–22, *120, 121,*
    122, 123
Wierdsma House, *109*
Wilson, Peter, 163
Wilton, N.Y.
    T-House, *8*

Windows, 27, 226
Window screens, 18, 27
Wolf House, 106, 126–29, *126, 127, 128, 129*
Wong, Kellogg, *82*
Wright, Frank Lloyd, 18, 52, 53, 105, 108, 150,
    198, 200
Wright Guest House, *166–67*
Wurster, William, 108

Yorktown, N.Y.
    Fitzpatrick House, *50, 51*

Carlos Zapata Design Studio
    Landes House, *6–7*

ACKNOWLEDGMENTS

A book such as this one is much like a Broadway play. There are a few onstage performers and a host of people working behind the scenes to make sure everything comes off smoothly.

In our case the performers are the four critics – Thomas Hine, Robert Campbell, Suzanne Stephens, and Charles Gandee – who wrote essays introducing each of the book's main sections. In addition to their roles as authors, they also helped select the houses included in the book, thereby laying the foundation stones for the final edifice. Their individual and combined wisdom on architecture informed the words and images found in the book you now hold.

Out of the limelight, a number of people were crucial to the inception and development of this book. Most important of all was Stephen A. Kliment, editor-in-chief of *Architectural Record* from 1990 to 1996, who had many years of experience in book publishing before coming to the magazine and who enthusiastically supported my efforts to mark the fortieth anniversary of *Record Houses* with a beautiful hardcover book. Simply put, this project would not have happened without Stephen's support and guidance.

The other editor at *Architectural Record* who provided expert advice and assistance was Karen D. Stein, the managing senior editor and editor-in-charge of *Record Houses* since 1993. Former editors of *Record Houses* who talked to me about the evolution of the publication and its role in the profession included Herbert L. Smith, Jr., who was the very first editor of the annual issue, Douglas Brenner, and Barclay Gordon.

At Harry N. Abrams, Inc., I am indebted to our editor Elisa Urbanelli, who not only helped shape a vision for the book but also provided the patient day-to-day care such a project requires. Another key player was Miko McGinty, who designed the book and made it a thing of beauty. In Abrams' publicity department, I must thank Carol Morgan, who championed the project when it was just a proposal, and Joanne Chaseman, who made sure the final book got the attention it deserves. And, of course, nothing happens at Abrams without the blessing and guidance of president, publisher, and editor-in-chief Paul Gottlieb.

As every Broadway director knows, you can have great actors and offstage help, but you need a good play with which to work. Our play tells the story of modern residential design – starting with the idealistic, somewhat delusional 1950s and ending with the less dogmatic but more chaotic 1990s. The playwrights are the architects who put their ideas to paper and created the houses that are the subject of this book. It's great material to work with. I would like to thank all of the designers working in all of the architectural offices who put their efforts into these houses. Behind all those architects are the artists who photographed the houses, translating three dimensions into two.

Finally, I must thank my wife Lily Chin, whose advice on people, process, and design helped me keep the project on track and my head on straight.

Clifford A. Pearson